DISTINCT
OR
EXTINCT

DISTINCT OR EXTINCT

Future-Proofing People & Organizations in the Age of AI

MIKE EVANS

*To my wife Despina, my sons, Nick and Zack,
and my stepchildren, Brady and Brooke,
who remind me every day that the future belongs to those
who prepare for it.*

*And to every professional asking,
"Will I be replaced?"
You won't—if you choose to be distinct.*

TABLE OF CONTENTS

THE PUBLISHER WHO NEEDED TO READ THIS BOOK

In January 2026, I pitched my completed manuscript to one of the world's largest business publishers. The meeting lasted ninety minutes. By the time I walked out, I knew three things with absolute certainty:

1. They didn't understand what I'd written.
2. They embodied every warning in my book.
3. They would have benefited enormously from actually reading it.

The irony was almost too perfect.

This book, the one you're holding right now, is about how organizations must adapt to survive disruption. How complacency kills companies. How arrogance blinds leaders to change happening all around them. How the difference between those who thrive and those who become extinct comes down to one simple choice. Will you see reality and respond, or will you cling to what worked yesterday?

The publisher sitting across from me couldn't see reality.

They looked at my manuscript, 243 pages of frameworks, stories, and strategies I'd developed over 27 years working with 34 Fortune 50 companies, and saw a commodity. Another 'AI book' in a crowded market. They made me feel ashamed that my first book, written in 2016 when I was a novice author, hadn't made them enough money. Never mind that it had successfully grown my speaking business to 40-60 keynotes annually with companies like Intel, Apple, Caterpillar, and PepsiCo. That wasn't their success, so it didn't count.

They wanted $60,000 upfront. They needed seven months to publish. They offered minimal support. When I asked what I'd actually receive for my investment, their answer was revealing: 'Credibility. You get credibility when we publish your book.'

Translation: Our logo is worth $60,000 to you.

That's complacency.
When I noted that self-publishing would cost me a fraction of their price while giving me complete control, faster time to market, and better margins, they were dismissive. This is how publishing works, they implied. This is how it's always worked. We're the publisher. Our process is our process.

That's inertia.
Throughout the meeting, there was an underlying tone of condescension. A subtle message that I should be grateful they were even considering my work. That I should recognize the honor of their interest. That my past 'underperformance' was a liability, not a learning experience.

That's arrogance.
Complacency. Inertia. Arrogance. Three powerful ingredients that weaken organizations and individuals until they can no longer compete. The publisher was drinking all three, yet they couldn't taste the poison.

• • •

Here's what made this moment profound: I wasn't angry. I was sad. Because I genuinely believed this publisher needed the message in my book.

Traditional publishing is collapsing. Self-publishing now accounts for an ever-growing share of book sales. Authors with established platforms increasingly choose independence over advances. The gatekeepers are losing their gates. Yet this publisher sat across from me, confident in their brand value, blind to the disruption reshaping their entire industry.

They needed to read Chapter 1 about the seven forces disrupting work as we know it. They needed Chapter 7 about how leadership either enables adaptation or prevents it. They needed the whole framework.

But they were too busy being a publisher to consider whether their publishing model still worked.

And here is the painful irony that crystallized for me on the drive home: In the same week I sat across from that publisher, 39 companies announced layoffs totaling more than 600,000 jobs. The CEO of Anthropic went on 60 Minutes and warned that AI could spike unemployment 10 to 20 percent within five years, naming lawyers, consultants, and finance professionals specifically. Jack Dorsey cut half of Block's workforce and called it a blueprint for the industry.

Three separate stories. One week. One unmistakable pattern. The forces I have been warning about for 27 years were no longer predictions. They were headlines.

The publisher couldn't see it. The question this book asks, and answers, is whether you can.

. . .

That night, I couldn't sleep. Not because I was anxious about the decision, I'd already decided to decline their offer. I couldn't sleep because the meeting had crystallized something important:

We judge organizations differently than we judge people.

In venture capital, investors value 'scar tissue.' An entrepreneur who failed once, or twice, or three times, is more attractive than someone succeeding on their first try. Why? Because failure teaches. It builds resilience. It reveals what works and what doesn't. Scar tissue equals wisdom.

Howard Schultz, the founder of Starbucks, pitched his vision for Il Giornale, which would become Starbucks, to 242 investors. He was rejected by 217 of them. An 89% rejection rate. Investors didn't believe Americans would pay premium prices for espresso drinks. They couldn't see past their assumptions about coffee culture.

Schultz didn't let their blindness become his burden. He found the 25 who could see what he saw. Today, Starbucks has over 32,000 locations worldwide.

But traditional publishers don't value scar tissue. They penalize past performance. My first book hadn't hit their sales targets, so I was damaged goods. Never mind that I'd learned. Never mind that this book was dramatically better. Never mind that I'd spent 11 additional years in the field, working with Fortune 500 clients on the exact disruption this book addresses.

Past results predicted future results. In their eyes, I was the entrepreneur who'd failed once. They couldn't see that failure is expensive tuition, not destiny.

. . .

THE CHOICE

So I made a choice.

I chose to practice what this book preaches. I chose adaptation over nostalgia. I chose to see reality clearly: I didn't need their logo. I needed speed to market, creative control, and margins that made sense. Most importantly, I needed to reach readers who are facing the same disruption I write about, before it's too late.

The publisher wanted seven months. I chose April. They wanted $60,000. I invested $10,000. They offered 'credibility.' I chose independence.

And you know what? That meeting became the opening story for this preface. Their inability to see their own disruption became validation of my thesis. Their condescension became my confidence.

Sometimes the best thing an organization can do for you is reject you. Because rejection clarifies what you already knew. You don't need permission to create value. You need courage to act on what you see.

I am not a speaker who discovered AI last year and rebranded overnight. I have been inside 34 Fortune 50 companies for 27 years, working alongside Dr. John Kotter, Dr. Stephen Covey, and Tom Peters, watching these forces build long before anyone called them disruption. What is happening right now is not a surprise to me. It is the convergence I have been mapping since 1998. And the defense I am about to share with you has been battle-tested across hundreds of organizations through every major disruption of the last three decades.

That is why this book exists now. Not because AI is new. Because the moment of urgency has arrived.

. . .

WHY I WROTE THIS BOOK

Over the past 27 years, I've worked with 34 Fortune 50 companies. I've delivered between 40 and 60 keynotes annually. I've worked alongside legendary thought leaders like Dr. John Kotter,

Dr. Stephen Covey, Tom Peters, and Jim Kouzes. I've been inside Intel, Apple, Caterpillar, PepsiCo, Capital One, and dozens more.

I've watched brilliant people lose their jobs because they couldn't see change coming. I've seen entire departments eliminated by software. I've witnessed once-dominant companies become irrelevant because they clung to strategies that worked yesterday. And I've seen others, individuals and organizations, not just survive but thrive by making one simple choice:

They chose to be distinct, not extinct.

This book exists because of a pattern I've observed for nearly three decades: The people and organizations that succeed aren't necessarily smarter, better funded, or more talented. They're more adaptively responsive. They see reality clearly. They move quickly. They invest in what matters. They differentiate themselves. And they lead, even when leading is uncomfortable.

But here's the problem: Most people don't see the threat until it's too late.

I call this threat the Seven-Sided Pincer Movement, seven massive forces converging simultaneously to disrupt work as we've known it. ERP systems and white-collar automation. Globalization and outsourcing. The internet and disruptive competition. And artificial intelligence, which amplifies every other force exponentially.

These seven forces aren't coming someday. They're here now. And they're accelerating.

In 1999, my mentor Tom Peters stood in front of a room of our clients and predicted that 90% of white-collar jobs would disappear or be fundamentally transformed within a decade. People thought he was being hyperbolic. He wasn't. He was early.

Marc Andreessen, co-founder of Netscape, predicted that by 2034, all traditional 9-to-5 jobs would be eliminated by technology. Ben Goertzel, a leading AI researcher, estimates that 80% of jobs are at risk from artificial intelligence. Ray Kurzweil predicts that by 2029, we'll connect our neocortex to the cloud, fundamentally changing human capability.

These aren't fringe voices. These are some of the most credible futurists and technologists in the world. And they're all saying the same thing:

The disruption is here. Adapt or become irrelevant.

. . .

WHAT MAKES THIS BOOK DIFFERENT

There are hundreds of books about artificial intelligence. Most focus on what's happening, the technology, the predictions, the fears. They describe the problem in fascinating detail.

This book is different.

This book focuses on what you do about it. Not someday. Right now. Today.

I don't just describe the threat. I give you the defense. I call it the Five-Ingredient Kryptonite, five specific, actionable strategies that make you and your organization resistant to disruption:

IDEAS: Mastery that sets you apart
SPEED: Agility that outpaces change
TALENT: Capability that can't be automated
DISTINCTION: Differentiation that makes you irreplaceable
LEADERSHIP: Influence that inspires others to adapt

These aren't theoretical concepts. These are battle-tested frameworks I've used with Fortune 50 companies for 27 years. They work for individuals. They work for teams. They work for entire organizations.

But here's what matters most: This book isn't just about surviving disruption. It's about thriving because of it. It's about seeing opportunity where others see threat. It's about building a career and an organization that becomes more valuable precisely because the world is changing.

Because here's the truth that most people miss. Disruption doesn't destroy value. Disruption redistributes value. It takes value away from those who refuse to adapt and gives it to those who see reality clearly and move decisively.

The question isn't whether you'll face disruption. You will.

The question is: Will you be distinct or extinct?

Those prepared need not fear the forces at work.

· · ·

WHO THIS BOOK IS FOR

This book is for anyone who suspects that the rules are changing but isn't quite sure what to do about it.

It's for the mid-career professional who's worried about their job becoming automated but doesn't know how to future-proof their career. It's for the executive watching competitors disrupt their industry and wondering how to respond. It's for the entrepreneur building something new in a landscape that shifts daily. It's for the team leader trying to keep their people engaged and adaptable in the face of constant change.

It's for the lawyer, the consultant, the finance professional who heard themselves named specifically on 60 Minutes and felt a chill. It's for the HR executive trying to figure out how to re-train a workforce faster than the disruption is moving. It's for the manager who knows their team is at risk but doesn't have a framework to act on that knowledge.

This book is for people who are willing to look reality in the face and do something about it.

If that's you, keep reading. Because what comes next could change everything.

. . .

A NOTE ABOUT THE PUBLISHER WHO SAID NO

I started this preface with that meeting for a reason. Not because I'm bitter, I'm not. Not because I want to criticize, I don't. But because that meeting perfectly illustrated the central tension in this book:

> *The hardest organizations to help are the ones*
> *who don't know they need help.*

That publisher genuinely believed their model still worked. They believed their brand still carried the weight it once did. They believed that an established author should feel grateful for their interest. They couldn't see that the ground beneath them had shifted.

Which means they're not villains. They're just human. And like all humans facing disruption, they defaulted to what worked before, prestige, process, precedent. They retreated to the comfort of their brand instead of confronting the reality of their market.

I tell this story not to shame them, but to remind you. If a major publishing house with vast resources and decades of experience can't see disruption coming for them, how much harder is it for you or me to see it coming for us?

That's why this book exists. To help you see. To give you the tools to respond. To show you that adaptation isn't just possible, it's the only sustainable path forward.

. . .

In Chapter 1, I'll introduce you to Mikey Calabrese, a Philadelphia longshoreman who never saw disruption coming, and Chen Wei, a port supervisor in Shanghai who did. Their stories, separated by 70 years and 7,000 miles, set up everything that follows.

By the end of this book, you'll understand exactly what separated them, and which path you're on. You'll have a clear roadmap to ensure you're one of the ones who thrives.

The choice is yours: Distinct or extinct.

Let's get started.

Mike Evans
Pittsburgh, Pennsylvania
March 2026

THE GHOST PORT

*Seeing the Future
Before It Arrives*

PHILADELPHIA, PENNSYLVANIA — OCTOBER 1956

Mikey Calabrese's alarm clock didn't get the chance to ring. It never did. Twenty years of loading cargo ships had wired his body to wake at 4:15 AM, fifteen minutes before the damn bell could shatter the quiet of his row house in South Philly.

He dressed in the dark, flannel shirt, dungarees, steel-toed boots that had molded to his feet like a second skin. Downstairs, the coffee was already percolating. Despina, his wife of twelve years, knew the routine as well as he did. She'd be asleep again before he hit the sidewalk.

The October air bit at his face as he walked the six blocks to Sal's Diner. Inside, the place hummed with the pre-dawn energy of men who worked with their bodies. Longshoremen, mostly. Some truck drivers. The occasional cop finishing a night shift.

"Mikey! Over here!" Big Eddie Kowalski waved from the corner booth, his massive frame taking up half the seat. Next to him sat Jimmy "The Weasel" DeMarco, so named because he could squeeze into cargo holds nobody else could reach.

Mikey slid in across from them. The waitress, Doris, been there twenty years, poured his coffee without asking.

"You see the board yet?" Eddie asked, his voice gravelly from too many Lucky Strikes.

"Not yet. What're we looking at?"

"Four ships. Dutch freighter in Pier 12, two Liberty ships on 34 and 35, and a big bastard container ship at 40. Word is the container's got machinery from Germany. Heavy lifts all day."

Mikey grinned. Heavy lifts meant overtime. Overtime meant he could get Despina that new washing machine she'd been eyeing at Gimbels. Maybe even take young Mikey Jr. to see the Phillies next spring.

"You think Donovan will put us on the container?" The Weasel asked.

"Better," Mikey said, tapping the table. "My cousin Vince said they need four gangs. We're all working today, boys."

By 6:00 AM, Pier 40 was organized chaos.

The SS Mercator sat low in the water, a 441-foot Dutch freighter loaded with 5,000 tons of automotive parts, industrial machinery, and precision equipment from Hamburg. Twenty-eight cargo holds. Roughly 180,000 cubic feet of freight that needed to move from ship to warehouse before the vessel could turn around and head back across the Atlantic.

Mikey's gang, twenty men strong, gathered around the hatch of Hold Number 3. Foreman Donovan, clipboard in hand and whistle around his neck, barked assignments.

"Calabrese, you're on the hook. Eddie, you and Martinez are in the hold. Weasel, you're running topside coordination. I want clean lifts, no damaged goods, no crushed fingers. The German stuff in this hold runs about two grand per crate. You drop it, you bought it."

Mikey climbed down into the hold, the smell of diesel fuel and ocean salt thick in his nostrils. The cargo was packed tight, wooden crates stamped with Deutsche Industrie labels, some as small as footlockers, others the size of automobiles.

The ballet began.

Men in the hold rigged the cargo nets. Mikey called signals up to the crane operator — a long blast for up, two short for stop, three for down. The winch groaned. The net rose, swaying slightly as it cleared the hatch. Topside, The Weasel guided it toward the waiting truck, where another crew unhooked and loaded.

One lift. Then another. Then another.

The rhythm was hypnotic. By 10:00 AM, they'd moved forty-three crates. By noon, eighty-seven. Mikey's shoulders burned. His hands, even through leather gloves, were raw from the cargo hooks.

They broke for lunch — sandwiches from home, thermoses of coffee, cigarettes. The men sat on the pier's edge, legs dangling over the water, watching the tugboats nudge a tanker into position three piers down.

"You know what I heard?" The Weasel said, unwrapping a meatball sandwich that smelled like heaven. "They're talking about making these containers standardized. Same size, so you can stack 'em like blocks."

Eddie snorted. "Yeah? And I heard they're gonna put a man on the moon. Load of horseshit."

"I'm serious. They're testing it in Newark. Big metal boxes, all the same dimensions. Crane picks up the whole box, drops it on a truck, truck drives away. No more rigging every piece."

Mikey chewed his bologna sandwich thoughtfully. "Even if they do that, they still need us. Somebody's gotta load the boxes, right? Somebody's gotta secure the cargo. Somebody's gotta run the cranes."

"Exactly," Eddie said. "My old man worked these docks. I'm working these docks. My kid'll probably work these docks. Some things don't change."

By 6:30 PM, when the shift whistle blew, they'd unloaded Hold Number 3 completely. Two hundred and fourteen crates. Twelve hours of back-breaking labor. The Mercator still had twenty-seven holds to go.

Mikey walked home in the dusk, every muscle screaming. His union card had gotten him $14.50 for the day — damn good money. In his pocket was a slip for Saturday overtime. The washing machine was practically bought.

At the dinner table, young Mikey Jr., nine years old, gap-toothed, full of questions, asked, "Dad, what'd you do today?"

"Moved mountains, buddy. One crate at a time."

"When I grow up, can I work the docks like you and Grandpa?"

Mikey looked at Despina, who smiled softly. He reached over and tousled his son's hair.

"Sure, kid. The docks'll always need strong backs and good men."

• • •

SHANGHAI, CHINA — OCTOBER 2024

Chen Wei's phone vibrated at 6:45 AM, his alarm set for a civilized hour compared to his grandfather's generation. He rolled out of bed in his apartment in Pudong, made green tea, and checked the overnight reports on his tablet while the subway carried him toward Yangshan Deep-Water Port.

Phase 4 of Yangshan was the most automated port in the world, and Chen was one of thirty-seven operations supervisors responsible for keeping it running. Where his grandfather, who'd worked the Shanghai docks in the 1970s, had supervised twenty men, Chen supervised two hundred and fourteen automated guided vehicles (AGVs), forty-seven automated ship-to-shore cranes, and exactly five human beings.

The control room was climate-controlled, quiet except for the hum of servers and the occasional radio chatter. Banks of monitors showed real-time feeds from across the port's four square miles. Chen's station displayed Hold Management for Berth 23, where the MSC Gülsün, the largest container ship in the world, had docked at 4:17 AM.

The Gülsün carried 23,756 TEUs — twenty-foot equivalent units. Each container was a standardized steel box, 20 or 40 feet long, stacked like LEGO blocks up to ten high on the deck. The ship was 400 meters long, longer than four football fields.

Chen logged into the Terminal Operating System. The AI had already generated the optimal discharge sequence — which containers to unload first based on destination, weight distribution, and the next port of call. The 3D visualization showed each container color-coded: red for immediate unload, yellow for secondary priority, green for restack.

He initiated the sequence.

On the dock, visible through the control room's panoramic windows, the automated cranes came to life. No human climbed into a crane cab. No one shouted signals. The cranes moved with eerie precision, their spreaders descending to lock onto containers, lifting them smoothly, swinging them over to the waiting AGVs.

The AGVs — looking like oversized Roombas with flatbeds — received their containers and glided silently toward the storage yard. No drivers. No horns. Just the whisper of electric motors and the orchestrated dance of machines.

Chen's job was to watch. The AI handled 97% of decisions. He intervened only when sensors flagged anomalies — a container weight mismatch, a crane reporting a mechanical fault, a traffic jam in the AGV lanes.

At 9:23 AM, his screen flashed yellow. Container MSCU-4782934 showed a weight discrepancy. Manifest said 18,000 kg. Scale said 22,000 kg.

Chen clicked the alert, initiated a hold, and sent a message to the customs AI. Probable misdeclared cargo. The container was automatically routed to inspection. The entire process took forty-seven seconds.

By 11:00 AM, the Gülsün was two-thirds unloaded. Where Mikey Calabrese's gang had moved 214 crates in twelve hours, Yangshan's automated systems had moved 15,000 containers in seven hours.

Chen ate lunch at his desk, takeout noodles, eyes on the screens. His colleague, Liu Yang, rolled her chair over.

"Did you see the email from headquarters?" she asked quietly.

"Which one?"

"The AI upgrade. Next quarter, they're implementing full autonomous operations for standard discharge sequences. No human oversight required unless the system flags critical errors."

Chen's stomach tightened. "What does that mean for staffing?"

Liu shrugged, but her eyes betrayed concern. "The memo said 'operational optimization.' You know what that means."

Chen did know. It meant fewer supervisors. It meant the five people in this control room might become three. Or two. Or one person just monitoring alerts.

"We're logistics professionals," Chen said, more to convince himself than Liu. "We have degrees. We understand the systems. They'll still need us."

"That's what the crane operators said ten years ago," Liu replied. "How many crane operators do you see now?"

Chen looked out the window at the forest of automated cranes. Not a single human operator among them.

By 6:00 PM, the Gülsün was completely unloaded. 23,756 containers, moved from ship to storage yard in thirteen hours and forty-one minutes. Average handling time per container: 2.1 seconds.

Chen logged out, rode the subway home, and found his eight-year-old daughter, Mei, doing homework at the kitchen table.

"Baba, what did you do today?" she asked.

Chen paused. What had he done? Watched screens. Clicked three alerts. Overridden one AI decision that turned out to be correct anyway.

"I supervised port operations," he said. "Made sure everything ran smoothly."

"Is that what you'll do when you're old like Grandpa?"

Chen thought about his grandfather, who'd died five years ago. The old man used to tell stories about moving cargo by hand, about the pride of physical work, about the certainty that his skills would always be needed.

"I don't know, Mei. Things change."

THE INVISIBLE TSUNAMI

Mikey Calabrese never saw it coming.

The standardized shipping container, that "load of horseshit" Eddie Kowalski dismissed in 1956, revolutionized global trade within a decade. By 1970, the Port of Philadelphia employed 8,000 longshoremen. By 1990, that number had dropped to 2,000. Today, it's fewer than 500.

The work didn't disappear. The cargo volume exploded. In 1956, US ports handled about 50 million tons of freight annually. Today, it's over 2 billion tons. But where it once took a gang of twenty men twelve hours to unload one hold, modern automated ports can unload entire mega-ships in less than a day.

Mikey's job, his identity, his family legacy, his son's assumed future, was automated out of existence. Not overnight. Not dramatically. Just steadily, inexorably, like a tide that never stopped rising.

**The displacement took thirty years.
Chen Wei's displacement is taking thirty months.**

I have spent 27 years studying these forces. Not 27 months. Not 27 weeks. The single most important thing that experience teaches is this: the people who insisted there was nothing to worry about were never the ones who adapted. They were the ones who disappeared.

The week I finished this manuscript, 39 companies announced layoffs totaling more than 600,000 jobs. The CEO of Anthropic went on 60 Minutes and warned that AI could spike unemployment 10 to 20 percent within five years — naming lawyers, consultants, and finance professionals specifically. Jack Dorsey cut half of Block's workforce and called it a blueprint for the industry.

Three separate stories. One week. One unmistakable pattern. What I have been warning about on stages since 1998 is no longer a prediction. It is a headline.

Here's what should get every worker's attention — whether you work with your hands, your mind, or both: Mikey worked with his hands. Chen works with his mind. You work with your mind.

To the forces of disruption, that distinction means nothing.

Mikey's replacement was visible. You could see the container cranes, the AGVs, the automation. The robots that took his job were mechanical, predictable, physical.

The forces displacing workers at every level are invisible, exponential, and already embedded in the systems your company runs on. It's in your email autocomplete. Your Excel formulas. Your data analytics platform. Your customer service chatbot. Your legal document review. Your code compiler. Your creative brief generator.

It's not coming. It's here.

But here's the critical difference between Mikey's story and yours: Mikey didn't have warning. You do.

Mikey couldn't have predicted that a simple standardized metal box would obsolete a labor force of millions. The technology seemed incremental — just a better way to pack cargo. By the time longshoremen understood they were facing existential disruption, the battle was already lost.

You're reading this book before your industry's Yangshan moment. Not after.

You're holding the warning Mikey never got.

The question is: What will you do with it?

THE 7-SIDED PINCER MOVEMENT

Mikey Calabrese was displaced by one primary force: automation and robotics in the form of containerization and mechanized cargo handling.

You're facing seven forces — all accelerating simultaneously, all converging on your role, your company, and your industry like a multi-front assault.

There are forces coalescing and joining together. They are coming to take our jobs from us. Coming to transform how departments operate. Coming to reinvent or destroy entire industries. This isn't fear-mongering. This is reality.

FORCE 1: Revolutionary Software (ERP, AI, Automation)

WHAT IT IS:

Enterprise software systems that fundamentally change how work gets done by automating processes, consolidating functions, and eliminating the need for human intervention in routine tasks.

THEN (1990S–2000S):

ERP systems — SAP, Oracle, PeopleSoft — eliminated entire departments. When companies implemented these systems, accounting, HR, and operations teams shrank by 30-60%. Jobs that once required specialists became automated workflows.

NOW (2020S):

AI-powered software doesn't just automate tasks — it makes decisions. RPA (Robotic Process Automation) tools handle invoice processing, customer service routing, compliance checking, and data entry with zero human involvement. No-code platforms let non-technical users build their own automation.

EMERGING:

AI assistants that can write code, design products, conduct research, and analyze markets. Tools like GitHub Copilot write 40% of code automatically. GPT-4 and Claude can draft legal documents, create marketing campaigns, and analyze financial statements.

IMPACT:

Entire job categories disappearing: data entry clerks, bookkeepers, administrative assistants
Middle management roles under pressure as software tracks performance automatically
The "productivity paradox": companies need fewer people to do more work
Speed advantage: What took weeks now takes minutes

FORCE 2: White-Collar and Blue-Collar Robots

WHAT IT IS:

Physical automation and robotic systems replacing human labor in manufacturing, logistics, service industries, and increasingly in knowledge work.

BLUE-COLLAR REVOLUTION:

ATMs eliminated 375,000 bank teller jobs. Amazon warehouses use 750,000 robots alongside humans. Self-checkout kiosks in retail. Automated car washes. Manufacturing robots in automotive plants. Construction robots laying bricks and welding. Agricultural robots picking fruit.

WHITE-COLLAR SURPRISE:

AI analyzing X-rays better than radiologists. Legal AI reviewing contracts faster than junior associates. Algorithmic trading replacing Wall Street analysts. Automated journalism — AP writes 3,000+ news stories per quarter using AI. ChatGPT writing code that would take developers days to create.

IMPACT:

47% of US jobs at risk of automation (Oxford University study)
The "hollowing out" effect: entry-level roles disappearing, making it harder to build careers
Blue-collar AND white-collar workers equally vulnerable
Speed and accuracy advantages that humans cannot match

FORCE 3: Globalization

WHAT IT IS:

The ability to access talent, resources, and markets anywhere in the world instantly, creating a truly global workforce competing for the same opportunities.

EXAMPLES:

Software engineers in India, Eastern Europe, and Latin America working for a fraction of US salaries
Virtual assistants in the Philippines handling customer service and admin work
Design teams in emerging markets competing for creative projects
Platforms like Upwork, Fiverr, and Toptal connecting companies with global talent instantly
Remote work accelerated by COVID making location irrelevant

IMPACT:

Your competition isn't the person in the next cubicle — it's someone in another country willing to work for less

Companies can hire "best athlete available" regardless of location

Time zones become advantages: work happens 24/7 across global teams

Cost pressure: Why pay $100/hour when you can get the same quality for $25/hour?

FORCE 4: Outsourcing

WHAT IT IS:

Contracting entire functions or processes to specialized external providers who can do it better, cheaper, and faster.

EXAMPLES:

Manufacturing outsourced to China, Vietnam, Mexico

Customer service outsourced to call centers in India and the Philippines

IT operations outsourced to managed service providers

HR functions (payroll, benefits) outsourced to ADP, Paychex

Marketing outsourced to agencies

Accounting outsourced to firms in India processing US tax returns overnight

IMPACT:

Entire departments eliminated: "Why have an IT department when we can outsource to experts?"

Career paths disrupted: functions that were ladders to management now outsourced

The "do more with less" pressure: remaining staff stretched thinner

Quality paradox: sometimes better results from specialists than generalists

FORCE 5: The Internet and Digital Disruption

WHAT IT IS:

The shift from physical to digital that eliminates intermediaries, physical locations, and traditional business models.

EXAMPLES:

Retail apocalypse: Sears, Toys R Us, Circuit City gone. Malls closing. Amazon dominates.

Banking: Mobile apps replacing branches. Millions of bank branch employees at risk.

Media: Newspapers decimated. Blockbuster gone. Streaming dominates.

Travel agents: Nearly extinct due to Expedia, Booking.com, direct booking

Real estate: Zillow and Redfin reducing need for agents

Education: Online courses replacing traditional instruction

IMPACT:

"Bye-bye brick and mortar" — entire industries restructured around digital models

The convenience factor: consumers choose ease over human interaction

Geographic boundaries erased: compete with everyone, everywhere

Information asymmetry eliminated: customers as informed as professionals

FORCE 6: Disruptive Competition

WHAT IT IS:

New business models and competitors that don't play by traditional industry rules, often decimating established players overnight.

EXAMPLES:

Uber/Lyft disrupted taxi industry (no cars, no drivers as employees)
Airbnb disrupted hotels (no properties owned)
Netflix disrupted Blockbuster (streaming vs. physical rentals)
Amazon disrupted retail (everything, everywhere, next-day delivery)
Tesla disrupted automotive (direct sales, electric, software-driven)
Venmo/PayPal disrupted banking (peer-to-peer payments)
Zoom disrupted business travel (why fly when you can video conference?)

IMPACT:

Tom Peters: "Banking is necessary. Banks are not."
Entire industries can be upended by a startup in a garage
First-mover advantage less important than fast-mover advantage
"The fast will eat the slow" — speed matters more than size
Asset-light models beat asset-heavy incumbents

FORCE 7: Artificial Intelligence (The Accelerant)

WHAT IT IS:

Machine learning and AI that doesn't just automate tasks but learns, adapts, decides, and creates — accelerating and amplifying all the other six forces.

EXAMPLES:

Medical AI diagnosing diseases from scans with higher accuracy than doctors

Legal AI: ROSS Intelligence reviewing millions of legal documents

Financial AI: Algorithmic trading, fraud detection, credit decisions

Creative AI: ChatGPT, DALL-E, Midjourney creating content, art, code

Customer service AI: chatbots handling 80% of routine inquiries

Hiring AI: algorithms screening resumes, conducting initial interviews

Self-driving vehicles: Waymo, Tesla eliminating driving jobs

THE ACCELERATION EFFECT:

Ben Goertzel (AI researcher): "There's an 80% chance AI will make most current jobs obsolete within a few years"

Marc Andreessen (venture capitalist): Predicts all 9-5 jobs eliminated by 2034

Ray Kurzweil (futurist, 86% prediction accuracy rate over 30 years): "A machine will be able to match human intelligence and go beyond it by 2029." Whether he is off by a year or five years, the question for every organization is the same: what is your plan?

Elon Musk: "If you have a super intelligent AI that is capable of writing incredibly well, convincing, constantly figuring out what is more convincing to people, and then it enters social media... how would we even know?" That question is no longer hypothetical.

The first six forces took decades. AI is happening in years, maybe months.

And if those predictions felt distant when you first picked up this book, consider what happened in a single week as I was completing this manuscript: 39 companies announced layoffs totaling more than 600,000 jobs. The CEO of Anthropic warned on national television that AI could spike unemployment 10 to 20 percent within five years. A major tech CEO cut half his workforce and called it a blueprint for the industry. Force 7 is not a forecast. It is a current event.

DO YOU SEE THE PATTERN?

Force 7 — Artificial Intelligence — isn't just another threat on the list. It's the accelerant that supercharges all the others:

AI makes Revolutionary Software smarter (Force 1)
AI makes Robots more capable (Force 2)
AI enables better global coordination (Force 3)
AI makes Outsourcing more effective (Force 4)
AI powers Digital platforms (Force 5)
AI enables new Disruptive models (Force 6)

The first six forces took decades to reshape industries. AI is compressing that timeline into years, maybe months.

The question isn't whether these forces will affect you. The question is: What happens when your competitors can access AI that amplifies every one of these advantages against you?

Each force alone would be challenging. Together, they form what I call the 7-Sided Pincer Movement — a coordinated attack on the status quo from every direction simultaneously.

Mikey faced one front. You're fighting seven.

But here's the truth that Mikey's story illuminates: Disruption doesn't announce itself. It doesn't ask permission. And by the time it's obvious to everyone, it's too late to adapt.

The longshoremen didn't lose their jobs because they weren't strong enough, skilled enough, or hard-working enough. They lost their jobs because the fundamental equation of value changed — and they didn't see it coming.

The white-collar equivalent is happening right now. Not in some distant future. Now.

Law firms are using AI to review contracts in seconds that used to take associates days. Marketing agencies are generating creative briefs with ChatGPT that used to require senior strategists. Financial analysts are being outperformed by machine learning algorithms. Radiologists are competing with AI that detects tumors they miss. Customer service departments are being replaced by chatbots that never sleep, never complain, and cost virtually nothing.

The equation of value is changing.

The question isn't whether you'll be affected. The question is whether you'll be prepared.

DISTINCT OR EXTINCT

Mikey Calabrese had three choices when containerization arrived:

1. Deny it. Pretend the changes weren't real, weren't permanent, weren't coming for him. Many longshoremen took this path. They fought to preserve the old ways, struck to protect obsolete work rules, and woke up one day to find themselves unemployable.

2. Survive it. Scramble for the shrinking pool of traditional jobs, accept diminished pay and status, cling to the edges of a dying profession. Some longshoremen did this — took early retirement, moved to smaller ports, accepted warehouse jobs at half the pay.

3. Evolve through it. Learn new skills, find new value, reinvent their role in a changed world. The few who did this — who became crane operators, logistics coordinators, port supervisors — not only survived but often thrived.

Most chose denial or survival. Very few chose evolution. And the reason is simple: Evolution requires seeing the threat before it's obvious, and acting before you're forced to.

*This book is your opportunity to choose evolution
while you still can.*

Chen Wei's story isn't over yet. He still has a job. He still has options. But the AI upgrade is coming next quarter, and he's starting to realize that his college degree, his technical skills, and his professional identity might not be enough.

Your story isn't over yet either.

You picked up this book, which means you sense something shifting. Maybe you've noticed AI doing tasks you used to do. Maybe you've watched your company automate processes that used to employ people. Maybe you've felt that low-grade anxiety that your expertise might not be as valuable as it used to be.

*That sense of unease? That's not paranoia.
That's pattern recognition. Trust it.*

Because here's what the longshoremen learned too late: The organizations and individuals who thrive through disruption aren't the strongest, the smartest, or the most experienced. They're the most adaptable.

They're the ones who see change coming and ask, "How do I evolve?" instead of "How do I stop this?"

They're the ones who make themselves distinct when everyone else is becoming extinct.

THE 5-INGREDIENT KRYPTONITE

Superman had one weakness: Kryptonite. A single element that could neutralize all his powers.

The 7-Sided Pincer Movement seems unstoppable — seven forces, all accelerating, all attacking simultaneously. How do you defend against that?

The answer isn't seven different strategies. It's not twenty different tactics. It's not a different response for each threat.

The answer is five ingredients that, when combined, create a personal and organizational Kryptonite to disruption — a defense so powerful that it doesn't just help you survive change, it positions you to dominate through it.

These five ingredients are:

1. IDEAS — The Innovation Imperative

Relentless focus on innovation, advancement, creativity, and challenging the process — not once, but continuously.
Complacency is a death sentence. Clinging to the status quo and standing still are the fastest pathways to irrelevance.
In the age of AI, if you're not innovating, you're already obsolete. You just don't know it yet.

2. SPEED — Velocity as Competitive Advantage

Embrace and cultivate true urgency — not panic, not false urgency, but genuine bias toward action.

The fast don't just beat the slow anymore. The fast eat the slow, digest them, and move on before the slow even realize the race has started.

Fast prototyping. Rapid iteration. Soar with successes, learn from failures, and move again before your competition catches their breath.

3. TALENT — Unleashing Human Capability

Draw out and leverage the unique talents of every person — embrace all perspectives, unlock hidden capabilities, and stop leaving potential on the table.

Develop new skills and competencies daily. You are the CEO of your life, your career, and your destiny. No one else is coming to save you.

In a world where AI can execute at machine speed, your distinct human capabilities — creativity, judgment, relationship-building, adaptive thinking — are your moat. Build them relentlessly.

4. DISTINCTION — Escaping the Sea of Sameness

Stand out in today's commoditized economy where everyone looks the same, sounds the same, and offers the same.

Gain vivid clarity on the Big 3: How are you Dramatically Different from every alternative? What is the Overt Benefit you bring that others cannot? How can you Prove it with evidence that's impossible to ignore?

Being "pretty good" at everything makes you invisible. Being exceptional at something specific makes you indispensable.

5. LEADERSHIP AT ALL LEVELS — Everyone Leads, No Exceptions

Draw out and cultivate the leadership capacity in everyone — leadership isn't a title, it's a choice to ask "What else can I do?" and then do it.

Instill a common shared vision of success that everyone can see, articulate, and pursue. Foster alignment, ownership, and accountability.

In the age of disruption, waiting for "leadership" to save you is a guaranteed path to extinction. Lead from wherever you are, or get left behind.

These aren't buzzwords. They're not feel-good concepts. They're the hard-edged competitive advantages that separated the long-shoremen who evolved from those who went extinct. They're what will separate Chen Wei from his colleagues when the next round of "operational optimization" hits. And they're what will separate you from your peers when AI comes for your industry.

The rest of this book is dedicated to showing you exactly how to build each ingredient — how to combine them into an impenetrable defense, and how to use that defense to go on offense. Not just to survive disruption, but to exploit it.

THE PROMISE

Before we get into the five ingredients, I want to tell you about one more thing waiting for you at the end of this book. In the appendix, you will find the Kryptonite Scorecard™, a self-assessment tool that measures where you stand today across all five ingredients and gives you an Integration Score that tells you how well your capabilities are working together. Think of it as your personal disruption readiness diagnostic. As you read each chapter, you will be building toward it. By the time you reach it, you will know exactly how to use it — and what to do with what it tells you.

Because here's the final lesson from Mikey Calabrese's story:

The future doesn't belong to those who had the most advantages in the past. It belongs to those who adapt fastest to what's coming next.

Mikey couldn't adapt. His world changed too fast, with too little warning, and no roadmap.

Chen Wei might adapt. He's starting to see the threat. He's not sure what to do yet.

You will adapt. Because unlike Mikey, you have warning. Unlike Chen, you're about to get the roadmap.

The Ghost Port of Yangshan — silent, efficient, nearly human-free — is both a warning and a promise.

The warning: This is coming for every industry, every profession, every comfortable assumption about how work gets done.

The promise is the one I have staked 27 years on.

Those prepared need not fear the forces at work.

Let's get prepared.

. . .

COMING UP IN CHAPTER 2:

In Chapter 2, we'll dive deep into the first side of the Pincer Movement: Artificial Intelligence and Machine Learning. You'll learn exactly what AI can and can't do, where it's headed in the next 18 months, and most importantly, how to position yourself on the right side of the disruption curve before your industry's Yangshan moment arrives.

The displacement is already happening. Let's make sure you're not on the wrong side of it.

THE TWO PATHS

*The 7-Sided Pincer Movement
and Your Choice*

THE CEO WHO SAW IT COMING

Sarah Chen sat in her corner office on the 42nd floor of a downtown Chicago high-rise, staring at the quarterly numbers on her screen. As CEO of a mid-sized insurance company, she'd seen her industry weather plenty of storms over her twenty-year career. But this was different.

Her Chief Technology Officer had just walked her through a demonstration of their new AI claims processing system. The AI could review and approve standard claims in 3.2 seconds. Her team of 47 claims adjusters averaged 26 minutes per claim.

The math was brutal.

"Sarah," her CTO had said carefully, "we could process our entire current volume with about eight people and the AI system. Maybe twelve if we want redundancy."

Forty-seven people down to eight. Some of those adjusters had been with the company for fifteen years. They were good at their jobs. They showed up every day. They followed the processes perfectly.

And they were about to become obsolete.

But here's what haunted Sarah as she looked out over the Chicago skyline: It wasn't just her claims adjusters. Her VP of Operations had mentioned that their new automated underwriting system would reduce that department by 60%. Her CFO was exploring AI-powered financial analysis that would eliminate most of the accounting staff. Even her marketing team — creative, innovative people — were being outperformed by AI content generators.

Sarah had a choice to make. Actually, she had dozens of choices to make. And every single one of them would determine whether her company, and the people who worked for it, would be distinct or extinct.

But the biggest question wasn't about technology or systems or efficiency.

The biggest question was: "How do I help my people
see what I'm seeing?"

I have sat across from hundreds of leaders asking that exact question. In boardrooms at Intel and Apple. In off-sites at PepsiCo and Caterpillar. In crisis sessions with companies that waited too long and transformation sessions with companies that moved just in time. For 27 years, across 34 Fortune 50 companies, it is the question that separates the organizations that adapt from the ones that disappear.

The answer is not a technology strategy. It is a belief strategy. And it starts with understanding the only two paths available when disruption arrives.

THE TWO PATHS: A TALE AS OLD AS DISRUPTION

Here's the uncomfortable truth about the 7-Sided Pincer Movement: Most people won't see it coming until it's too late.

Not because they're stupid. Not because they're lazy. Not because they don't care about their careers or their companies.

They won't see it coming because of how human beings are wired to respond to threats and change.

When faced with disruption — whether it's AI replacing your job, your industry being reinvented, or your expertise becoming obsolete — every person and every organization splits down one of two paths:

PATH 1: INTERNALIZE

PATH 2: EXTERNALIZE

Which path you choose will determine everything.

Path 1: Internalize — *"What Can I Control?"*

People who internalize ask a fundamentally different question when disruption hits: "What can I do about this?"

They don't deny the threat. They don't pretend it's not real. They don't wait for someone else to fix it.

They look in the mirror and ask:

What skills do I need to develop?
How can I add value in this new reality?
What can I control in this situation?
Where's the opportunity hidden in this disruption?

These are the people who see AI coming and think, "How do I become the person who works WITH AI to do things neither of us could do alone?"

These are the organizations that see automation and think, "How do we redeploy our talent to higher-value work?"

These are the leaders who see the 7-Sided Pincer Movement and think, "How do we turn these forces into competitive advantages?"

Internalizers don't have perfect information. They don't know exactly what's coming. But they operate from a position of agency — the belief that their choices matter, their actions have impact, and their future is something they can influence.

They're not Pollyannas. They're realists with a bias toward action.

Internalization in Action:
The Regional Bank That Chose to Evolve

In 2019, a regional bank in the Midwest faced a brutal reality: their traditional retail banking business was dying. Branch traffic was down 40% in five years. Mobile banking had gutted their competitive advantage. Fintech startups were eating their lunch on loans and deposits.

The executive team had a choice.

They could externalize: Blame the fintechs. Blame the regulators. Blame customer disloyalty. Lobby for protection. Complain about unfair competition. Cut costs and hope to survive long enough for things to "go back to normal."

Or they could internalize.

They chose internalization.

The CEO stood up in a town hall and said something remarkable: "The world doesn't owe us a living. Our customers don't owe us their business. We have to earn it every single day. And right now, we're not earning it. So here's what we're going to do: We're going to become so good at understanding our customers' financial lives that no algorithm can compete with us."

They didn't fire their branch staff. They retrained them as financial wellness advisors. They didn't eliminate their loan officers. They repositioned them as trusted guides through life's major financial decisions. They didn't slash their technology budget. They invested heavily in AI tools that made their people smarter, faster, and more insightful.

Three years later, they'd grown deposits by 23%, increased customer satisfaction scores by 40%, and — here's the number that tells the real story — increased employee engagement scores by 52%.

Same industry. Same disruption. Different choice.
They internalized.

Path 2: Externalize — "It's Not My Fault"

People who externalize ask a very different question when disruption hits: "Who's to blame for this?"

They look everywhere except in the mirror:

It's the economy.
It's the regulators.
It's the competitors who don't play fair.
It's the technology that's moving too fast.
It's the customers who don't appreciate quality anymore.
It's the executives who don't understand the business.
It's the board that won't invest properly.

Externalizers aren't necessarily wrong about the challenges. The economy might actually be tough. The regulators might actually be creating barriers. The technology might actually be moving too fast.

But here's the fatal flaw in externalization:

*If it's not your fault, it's also not in your control.
And if it's not in your control, there's nothing you can do
about it except complain, hope, and wait.*

Externalizers become victims of their circumstances. And victims don't thrive. They survive, barely, or they go extinct.

Externalization in Action:
The Taxi Medallion Owner

In 2010, a taxi medallion in New York City was worth $1.3 million. By 2020, it was worth $200,000. By 2023, some were selling for under $100,000.

Why? Uber. Lyft. The ride-sharing revolution.

Now, here's what's fascinating: Taxi drivers and medallion owners saw Uber coming years before it destroyed their business model. They had time. They had resources. They had intimate knowledge of the transportation market.

How did most respond? Externalization.

They sued. They lobbied. They protested. They demanded that regulators shut down the "illegal" competition. They insisted that customers would "come to their senses" and realize that licensed taxis were safer, more professional, better.

They blamed Uber for not playing by the rules. They blamed the regulators for not enforcing existing laws. They blamed customers for being cheap and short-sighted.

What they didn't do — with very rare exceptions — was internalize and ask:

How can we compete on convenience?
How can we match the technology experience?

How can we turn our advantages — licensed, professional, local knowledge — into a premium service?
How can we create value Uber can't replicate?

A handful of taxi companies did internalize. They built apps. They created premium services. They focused on corporate clients and specific niches where their strengths mattered.

Those companies survived. Some even thrived.

The rest? They're still driving taxis, making a fraction of what they used to make, angry at a world that moved on without them.

Externalization feels good in the moment — it absolves you of responsibility, gives you someone to blame, creates solidarity with other victims.

But it is a death sentence in the age of disruption.

WHY WE EXTERNALIZE: THE RESULTS MODEL

If externalization is so obviously destructive, why do so many smart people — smart organizations — choose that path?

The answer lies in understanding how human beings create their reality. I call it the Results Model, and once you understand it, you'll see why 70% of change initiatives fail — and more importantly, how to be in the 30% that succeed.

THE RESULTS MODEL

EXPERIENCES → BELIEFS → ACTIONS → RESULTS

EXPERIENCES:

Everything that happens to you and around you. The economy, your boss, your colleagues, your successes, your failures, your family, the news, your industry, technology changes — everything.

BELIEFS:

The stories you tell yourself about what your experiences mean. This is where things get interesting — and dangerous.

ACTIONS:

What you actually do (or don't do) based on your beliefs.

RESULTS:

The outcomes you get from your actions.

And here's the critical part that most people miss:

> *Your results become your next experiences — creating a self-reinforcing loop that either lifts you or buries you.*

• • •

The Results Model is worth holding onto as you move through the rest of this book. When you reach the Kryptonite Scorecard in the appendix, you will be assessing your Actions, the specific behaviors you demonstrate consistently across five ingredients. But remember, those behaviors are downstream of your Beliefs, and your Beliefs were shaped by your Experiences. If your scores come back lower than you expected, the question to ask is not just 'what am I doing wrong?' It is 'what do I believe about innovation, speed, talent, distinction, and leadership that is producing these behaviors?' That is where the real work lives. The Scorecard shows you the Actions. The Results Model shows you why they are what they are.

. . .

The Externalize Loop: A Downward Spiral

Imagine you're a mid-level manager at a manufacturing company. AI and automation are starting to eliminate roles in your department.

EXPERIENCE: You see three colleagues laid off. You watch their jobs absorbed by automated systems.

BELIEF (Externalize): *"The company doesn't value people anymore. Technology is taking over and there's nothing I can do about it. Loyalty doesn't matter. I'm probably next."*

ACTION: You stop volunteering for new projects. You do the minimum required. You update your resume but don't develop new skills because "what's the point?" You complain to colleagues about how the company is changing.

RESULTS: Your performance declines. You're not on the radar for advancement. When the next round of cuts comes, you're on the list because you haven't made yourself indispensable.

NEW EXPERIENCE: You get laid off.

NEW BELIEF: *"See? I told you. Companies don't care about people. The system is rigged. Technology destroys jobs."*

And the cycle continues — stronger this time — as you carry those beliefs into your job search, your next role, your career.

This is the Externalize Loop. And it's devastating because:

The beliefs feel true (you really did get laid off)
The beliefs are self-confirming (your actions based on those
  beliefs created the result)
The beliefs feel justified (you have "evidence")

*But here's what you miss: Your beliefs — not the circumstances —
drove your results.*

The Internalize Loop: An Upward Spiral

Now let's replay the same scenario with internalization:

EXPERIENCE: You see three colleagues laid off. You watch their jobs absorbed by automated systems. (Same experience.)

BELIEF (Internalize): *"The company is changing fast. Roles that can be automated will be. I need to become someone who can't be automated. I need to add value in ways the machines can't. I need to learn how to work with AI, not compete against it."*

ACTION: You volunteer to learn the new AI systems. You identify ways to use automation to do your current job faster so you can take on higher-value work. You position yourself as the bridge between the technology and the people. You become the expert others come to for help.

RESULTS: You're seen as adaptable, forward-thinking, valuable. When reorganization happens, you're not on the cut list — you're on the "essential talent we need to build around" list. You might even get promoted to lead the transformation.

NEW EXPERIENCE: You survived the disruption and emerged stronger.

NEW BELIEF: *"I can navigate change. I can adapt. I have agency. When disruption comes, I can figure it out."*

And the cycle continues — stronger this time — as you carry those beliefs into the next disruption, making you even more resilient.

This is the Internalize Loop. And it's powerful because:

The beliefs feel true (you really did adapt successfully)
The beliefs are self-confirming (your actions based on those beliefs created the result)
The beliefs are justified (you have "evidence")

Your beliefs — not the circumstances — drove your results.
The same is true whether you internalize or externalize.

THE CRITICAL INSIGHT: SAME EXPERIENCE, DIFFERENT BELIEFS, DIFFERENT RESULTS

Do you see it?

Two people. Same company. Same disruption. Same layoffs. Same AI implementation.

Radically different outcomes.

Not because one was smarter. Not because one was luckier. Not because one had better skills to start with.

Because one internalized and one externalized.

The internalizer looked at the experience and asked, "What can I do?"

The externalizer looked at the experience and asked, "Who's to blame?"

The internalizer believed they had agency.

The externalizer believed they were a victim.

The internalizer took action based on what they could control.

The externalizer took action based on what they couldn't control — complaining, hoping, blaming.

And both were right — about themselves.

WHY ORGANIZATIONS FAIL TO CHANGE: THE COLLECTIVE RESULTS MODEL

Now let's scale this up. Because the Results Model doesn't just apply to individuals — it applies to entire organizations.

When the 7-Sided Pincer Movement hits your company, your organization will collectively develop beliefs about what it means.

Externalizing Organization

BELIEFS:

"Our industry is different — this won't affect us the same way"
"We can't compete with tech companies on technology"
"Our customers value relationships, not efficiency"
"Regulation will protect us"
"This is a fad — it'll blow over"
"We need to wait and see what happens"

ACTIONS:

Incremental changes instead of transformation
Committees and task forces instead of action
Defending the status quo instead of reinventing
Cutting costs instead of investing in capability
Waiting for the market to prove the threat is real

RESULTS:

Market share erosion
Talent exodus — the best people leave first
Innovation deficit
Eventually: irrelevance or acquisition

The data on this is striking. Cisco's internal research from their People Intelligence team shows that employees whose direct leaders actively use AI are twice as likely to adopt AI themselves. When leaders externalize — treating AI as someone else's problem, waiting for headquarters to mandate it, avoiding the tools themselves — adoption across their teams collapses. The externalization doesn't stay at the top. It cascades. An externalizing leader builds an externalizing organization, one department at a time.

Internalizing Organization

BELIEFS:

"We can't stop this, but we can ride it"
"Our competitors face the same forces — advantage goes to whoever adapts fastest"
"We have strengths we can amplify with these new tools"
"Our people are capable of more than we're asking of them"
"The future belongs to those who build it"

ACTIONS:

Bold experimentation with new models
Rapid deployment of new capabilities
Redefining value proposition
Investing in people and technology simultaneously
Moving before they have perfect information

RESULTS:

Market leadership in the new landscape

Talent magnetism — the best people want to be part of the transformation

Innovation advantage

Eventually: dominance

This is why Sarah Chen's question — "How do I help my people see what I'm seeing?" — is the most important question a leader can ask.

Because if her organization develops externalizing beliefs about the AI disruption, no amount of technology investment will save them.

But if she can help her organization develop internalizing beliefs — "We can figure this out, we have agency, our choices matter" — then they have a chance not just to survive but to dominate.

THIS IS NOT A THOUGHT EXPERIMENT

The week I completed this manuscript, 39 companies announced layoffs totaling more than 600,000 jobs. In the same week, the CEO of Anthropic went on 60 Minutes and warned that AI could spike unemployment 10 to 20 percent within five years — naming lawyers, consultants, and finance professionals specifically. Jack Dorsey cut half of Block's workforce and publicly called it a blueprint for the industry.

Then Oracle announced it was cutting 20,000 to 30,000 employees. Not because the company was struggling — its contracted future revenue had grown 433 percent year over year. Oracle was making a deliberate trade: people for AI infrastructure. One internal pilot program had already replaced 47 database administrators with three senior architects overseeing automated systems.

Implementation timelines that once took six weeks were running in approximately six hours. Oracle is not a startup making desperate bets. It is a 47-year-old institution that serves the data infrastructure of corporate America. When a company like that makes that kind of trade, it is not a warning. It is a policy.

Watch how organizations and individuals are responding to those headlines. Some are internalizing: asking what they need to learn, how they need to evolve, what value they can create that AI cannot. Others are externalizing: complaining that it's unfair, demanding regulation, insisting their industry is different, hoping it passes.

The Results Model is running in real time, right now, in every organization in the world. The question is which loop your organization — and you — are in.

Because 27 years of watching disruption cycles has taught me one thing with absolute certainty: by the time externalization feels wrong, it is usually too late to course-correct.

THE CHOICE IN FRONT OF YOU

So here's where we are:

You've seen the 7-Sided Pincer Movement. You know the forces converging on your role, your company, your industry. You've met Mikey Calabrese and Chen Wei. You understand that the displacement is real, it's accelerating, and it's coming for white-collar work with the same inevitability that it came for blue-collar work.

Now you have a choice.

You Can Externalize:

Blame AI for being unfair
Blame your company for not protecting you
Blame your industry for changing too fast
Blame education systems for not preparing you
Blame regulators for not stopping it

If you choose this path, you'll have plenty of company. You'll find solidarity with other victims. You'll have righteous anger on your side. You'll be "right" about all the unfairness.

And you'll go extinct.

Or You Can Internalize:

Accept that disruption is real and it's here
Acknowledge that your old advantages may not matter anymore
Recognize that you have agency — your choices matter
Ask "What can I do?" instead of "Who's to blame?"
Focus on what you can control
If you choose this path, it won't be easy. You won't have all the answers. You'll have to learn new things, let go of old identities, embrace uncertainty.

And you'll become distinct.

The choice seems obvious when written out like this. Of course internalization is better than externalization. Of course agency is better than victimhood. Of course adaptation is better than blame.

But here's why this is hard:

Your brain doesn't want you to internalize. Your brain wants you to externalize. Because externalization protects your ego, preserves your identity, and absolves you of the hard work of change.

Internalization requires you to admit that some of your current skills might not matter anymore. It requires you to question beliefs you've held your whole career. It requires you to do things you've never done before.

That's uncomfortable. That's scary. That's why most people don't do it until they're forced to — and by then, it's often too late.

THE GOOD NEWS: YOU CAN CHANGE YOUR BELIEFS

Here's what I've learned working with thousands of leaders and professionals over 27 years:

Your current beliefs aren't permanent. They're not hardwired. They're not your destiny.

Beliefs are just stories you've told yourself based on your experiences. And like any story, they can be rewritten.

The question is: What story are you going to tell yourself about the 7-Sided Pincer Movement?

Are you going to tell yourself a story of inevitability and victimhood? "This is happening to me and there's nothing I can do about it."

Or are you going to tell yourself a story of agency and adaptation? "This is happening around me and I get to choose how I respond."

The rest of this book is designed to help you write the internalization story. To give you the frameworks, tools, strategies, and confidence to look at the 7-Sided Pincer Movement and think:

"I've got this. I can figure this out. I can become someone the disruption can't touch."

But first, you have to make the choice.

Internalize or externalize.
Agency or victimhood.
Distinct or extinct.

Choose wisely. Because as Mikey Calabrese learned too late, and as Chen Wei is learning right now:

The future doesn't wait for you to be ready. It doesn't ask permission. And it doesn't care which story you tell yourself.

It just happens.

Those prepared need not fear the forces at work.
The only question is: Will you be ready when it does?

. . .

COMING UP IN CHAPTER 3:

Now that you understand the two paths and the Results Model that drives them, we're going to dive into the first ingredient of your Kryptonite defense: IDEAS.

You'll learn why innovation isn't optional anymore, how to challenge the process without getting fired, and most importantly, how to develop the idea-generation muscle that makes you indispensable in a world where AI can execute faster than any human.

Because here's the truth: AI can optimize. AI can execute. AI can analyze.

But AI can't dream. It can't imagine what doesn't exist yet. It can't challenge assumptions it doesn't know it has.

That's your advantage — if you learn how to use it.

THE 5-INGREDIENT KRYPTONITE DEFENSE

IDEAS

*The First Ingredient
of Your Kryptonite Defense*

THE ENGINEER WHO SAW AROUND CORNERS

In 1997, a young software engineer named Reed Hastings returned a copy of Apollo 13 to his local Blockbuster Video in Scotts Valley, California. The tape was six weeks overdue. The late fee was $40.

Standing at the counter, wallet open, paying a penalty that was more than the cost of buying the VHS tape outright, Reed had an idea.

Not a small idea. Not an incremental improvement idea. Not a "let's make the late fee system slightly less painful" idea.

A complete reimagining idea.

He thought: "What if there were no late fees? What if you could keep movies as long as you wanted? What if video rental worked like a gym membership — pay one monthly fee, unlimited access?"

That idea became Netflix.

But here's what's fascinating: Reed's idea wasn't about technology. The internet was barely capable of streaming video in 1997. Netflix started as a DVD-by-mail service — a business model that sounds hilariously antiquated today.

The idea was about reimagining customer experience. It was about challenging an assumption everyone in the video rental industry had accepted as gospel: late fees are how we make money.

Blockbuster had 9,000 stores at its peak. They employed over 80,000 people. They generated $6 billion in annual revenue. They were the dominant player in a massive, stable industry.

And they went extinct because they couldn't imagine a world without late fees.

Reed Hastings had one idea. One big, audacious, customer-centric idea that challenged the fundamental business model of an entire industry.

That's the power of IDEAS. That's the first ingredient of your Kryptonite defense.

I have watched this pattern play out for 27 years inside 34 Fortune 50 companies. The organizations that survived disruption were never the ones with the biggest budgets or the most established brands. They were the ones with the most relentless culture of idea generation — the ones that never stopped asking "what if" even when things were going well. The organizations that went extinct were the ones that confused execution excellence with strategic immunity. Blockbuster executed brilliantly right up until the moment it didn't matter anymore.

That distinction — between executing well and imagining differently — is the difference this chapter is about.

WHY AI MAKES IDEAS MORE VALUABLE, NOT LESS

Here's the paradox that confuses people about the AI revolution:

As machines get better at execution, human ideas become MORE valuable, not less.

Let me explain why.

AI is extraordinary at optimization. Give it a task, a dataset, and clear parameters, and it will find the most efficient path to the goal faster than any human could. It can write code, analyze data, generate content, process claims, draft contracts, create marketing copy, and do a thousand other tasks with speed and accuracy that makes human performance look glacial.

But AI has a fatal limitation: It can only optimize within the boundaries you give it.

AI can't question whether the boundaries make sense. It can't imagine a completely different game. It can't challenge the fundamental assumptions underlying the task.

AI could have made Blockbuster's late fee collection system incredibly efficient. It could have optimized store locations. It could have predicted which movies to stock based on local demographics. It could have created targeted marketing campaigns to drive traffic.

But AI would never have imagined Netflix.
Because Netflix required someone to ask a question AI can't ask:
What if the entire business model is wrong?

THE EXECUTION/IMAGINATION GAP

Think of it this way:

AI is the ultimate executor. Give it a well-defined problem and it will solve it brilliantly. It's the best employee you've ever had for structured, repeatable tasks.

But humans are the ultimate imaginers. We can see problems that don't exist yet. We can invent solutions to problems others don't see. We can challenge assumptions that everyone else accepts as reality.

This creates what I call the Execution/Imagination Gap — and it's widening every day.

THE EXECUTION / IMAGINATION GAP

EXECUTION (AI Domain)

Optimize existing processes
Execute defined tasks faster
Find patterns in existing data
Improve efficiency within current models
Scale proven approaches

IMAGINATION (Human Domain)

Question fundamental assumptions
Envision entirely new possibilities
Combine unrelated concepts from different domains
Challenge 'the way we've always done it'
Create what doesn't exist yet

As AI takes over more of the Execution domain, the value of the Imagination domain skyrockets.

Ben Goertzel, one of the world's leading AGI researchers, put it plainly: humans are not that general in the scope of all possible general intelligences. He is right. Stop competing in AI's 755 dimensions. That race is over before it starts. The human advantage lives somewhere AI cannot follow — in the ability to imagine what does not yet exist, to question what everyone else accepts, and to feel what no algorithm can feel.

This is not a philosophical point. It is a strategic one. In the same week I finished this manuscript, 39 companies announced more than 600,000 layoffs driven by AI automation. The Anthropic CEO warned on national television that lawyers, consultants, and finance professionals are specifically at risk. Every one of those layoffs was in the Execution domain — roles AI can now perform faster, cheaper, and at scale. The Imagination domain remains untouched. The question is whether you are building your value there.

The people who will thrive in the age of AI aren't those who can execute faster — they're those who can imagine better.

THE PRODUCT MANAGER WHO BECAME INDISPENSABLE

Let me tell you about Jessica, a product manager at a mid-sized software company in Austin, Texas.

In 2022, her company introduced AI tools that could do most of her analytical work. The AI could analyze user data, identify patterns, generate feature recommendations, even draft product requirement documents. Tasks that used to take Jessica days now took minutes.

She watched three of her peers get laid off. All of them were good at their jobs. All of them knew the products cold. All of them could execute flawlessly.

But they were all doing work that AI could now do better, faster, and cheaper.

Jessica took a different path. While her colleagues were fighting to prove they could analyze data faster than AI — they couldn't — Jessica started asking different questions:

What problems are our customers experiencing that they don't
    even know they have yet?
What if we completely reimagined how our product gets used?
What adjacent markets could we serve with our core technology?
What assumptions about our industry are probably wrong?

She wasn't trying to compete with AI on execution. She was operating in territory AI couldn't touch: imagination.

Six months later, Jessica had become the most valuable person on her team. Not because she could analyze data better than AI — she couldn't. Not because she could write requirements documents faster — she couldn't.

She was valuable because she had ideas. Big ideas. Unexpected ideas. Ideas that challenged assumptions. Ideas that opened new markets. Ideas that competitors hadn't thought of yet.

> *"Jessica went from being a good executor to being irreplaceable.*
> *We can train AI to do analysis. We can't train it to imagine*
> *new possibilities the way she does."*

That's the power of IDEAS in the age of AI.

THE THREE TYPES OF IDEAS THAT MATTER

Not all ideas are created equal. In my 27 years working with Fortune 50 companies, I've seen thousands of ideas proposed. Most go nowhere. Some create incremental value. A few change everything.

The ideas that matter — the ones that make you indispensable in the age of AI — fall into three categories.

Type 1: Assumption-Challenging Ideas

These are ideas that question the fundamental beliefs everyone in your industry, your company, or your role takes for granted.

"What if late fees aren't necessary?" (Netflix)
"What if hotel rooms didn't need to be in hotels?" (Airbnb)
"What if cars didn't need drivers?" (Tesla, Waymo)
"What if phones didn't need keyboards?" (iPhone)
Every industry, every company, every role has sacred cows — things everyone believes to be true, necessary, or unchangeable. Assumption-Challenging Ideas question those sacred cows.
In your role, ask yourself:
What does everyone in my industry assume is necessary that might not be?
What problem are we solving that customers don't actually care about?
What if the opposite of our core belief is true?
What 'rule' exists only because 'we've always done it that way'?

I worked with a manufacturing company where everyone assumed customers wanted faster delivery. It was the company religion. Millions invested in logistics optimization. AI systems to route shipments. Overnight delivery promises.

Then someone asked an assumption-challenging question: "What if customers don't actually care about speed? What if they care about predictability?"

They tested it. Turns out, customers were fine with five-day delivery if they knew exactly when the product would arrive and it actually arrived then. But they hated two-day delivery that showed up on day four without warning.

One assumption-challenging question, backed by simple testing, redirected millions in investment and dramatically improved customer satisfaction. It took zero AI to ask that question. It took a human willing to challenge what everyone 'knew' to be true.

Type 2: Connection-Creating Ideas

These are ideas that combine concepts, technologies, or approaches from different domains in unexpected ways.

Steve Jobs famously said the iPhone came from combining a phone, an iPod, and an internet communicator. But the real innovation was adding a touch interface from another domain entirely — tablets and PDAs — and making it the primary interaction model.

AI can analyze patterns within a domain brilliantly. But it struggles to make creative leaps across domains because it doesn't have the broad, unstructured experience of living in the world the way humans do.

Connection-Creating Ideas happen when you ask:

What's working in a completely different industry that we could adapt here?

What technologies exist in another field that could solve our problem?

What if we combined our core strength with an approach from another domain?
Who's solving a similar problem in a completely different context?

A healthcare client was struggling with patient compliance — people not taking medications as prescribed. They'd tried everything in the healthcare playbook: better instructions, reminder systems, educational programs. Nothing moved the needle significantly.

Then someone asked: "How does the gaming industry keep people engaged with daily habits?"

They brought in expertise from mobile game design, loyalty programs, and behavioral psychology from consumer apps — and created a medication adherence program that used gamification principles. Compliance rates jumped 40%.

The idea wasn't harder. It was just connected differently.
And AI, trained on healthcare data, would never have suggested
borrowing from mobile gaming because AI doesn't make those
lateral leaps naturally.

Type 3: Customer-Obsessed Ideas

These are ideas that start from a deep understanding of what customers actually experience — not what we think they experience.

Reed Hastings' late fee story is a perfect example. Blockbuster saw late fees as a revenue stream. Reed saw them as the customer's pain point.

AI can analyze customer data at scale. It can identify patterns in purchasing behavior, usage metrics, support tickets. But it can't feel the frustration of paying a $40 late fee. It can't experience the anger, the embarrassment, the sense of being punished for a minor mistake.

Customer-Obsessed Ideas come from empathy — from putting yourself in the customer's shoes so completely that you feel their pain and imagine their delight.

These ideas answer the question:

What frustrates our customers that they've just accepted as normal?
What job is the customer really trying to do (versus what we think they're doing)?
What would make this experience delightful instead of merely functional?
If we could start over knowing what we know now, would we design it this way?

I worked with a credit union that was struggling to compete with big banks on digital features. The banks had bigger budgets, better AI, faster apps. The credit union could never win the execution race. So they stopped trying.

Instead, someone asked: "What do our members hate about banking that they've just accepted as normal?"

The answer came back clear: They hate calling customer service and navigating phone trees. They hate being treated like account number 8675309.

So the credit union did something radical. They gave every member a direct phone number to a real human who knew their account. No phone tree. No hold music. No 'press 1 for...' Just call — and a human answers who knows who you are.

Was it efficient? No. Was it scalable with AI? Not really. Did it make members insanely loyal? Absolutely.

That's a Customer-Obsessed Idea. It challenged the industry assumption that efficiency matters more than humanity. And it created distinction in a sea of sameness.

BUILDING YOUR IDEA MUSCLE: FROM EXECUTOR TO IMAGINER

Here's the bad news: Most people are trained to be idea consumers, not idea creators.

We're taught to execute the plan, follow the process, implement the strategy that someone else developed. We're rewarded for reliability, consistency, and following instructions. We're punished for coloring outside the lines.

By the time most people reach mid-career, they've had the idea muscle trained out of them.

The good news? You can rebuild it. Ideas aren't magic. They're a skill. And like any skill, they get stronger with practice.

Practice 1: The Daily Question Ritual

Every single day, ask yourself one powerful question about your work:

"What if we did the opposite?"

Take whatever your team, your department, or your company is doing and imagine the opposite. Don't worry about whether it's practical. Don't censor yourself. Just explore the opposite.

If you're trying to acquire MORE customers, what if you focused on serving FEWER customers better?

If your strategy is to launch products faster, what if you launched slower but with deeper customer insight?

If your meetings are getting longer, what if you made them radically shorter — or eliminated them entirely?

If you're trying to reduce costs, what if you increased investment in the right places?

Most 'opposite' ideas won't work. That's fine. You're not trying to implement them. You're trying to challenge your assumptions — to see your work from a completely different angle.

But here's what happens: About once a week, maybe once a month, an 'opposite' question will surface an assumption you didn't know you were making. And that assumption, once questioned, opens up entirely new possibilities.

That's how Assumption-Challenging Ideas are born.

Practice 2: The Cross-Pollination Hunt

Once a week, deliberately expose yourself to a completely different domain:

Read an article about an industry you know nothing about. Watch a documentary about a topic you've never explored. Attend a meetup for a profession totally different from yours. Have lunch with someone whose job you don't understand.

Then ask yourself: "What are they doing that we could adapt?"

The healthcare company that borrowed from gaming? That came from someone who played mobile games with their kid and thought, "I wonder if these engagement mechanics could work for medication adherence?"

The credit union with direct phone numbers? That came from someone who stayed at a boutique hotel where the concierge knew every guest by name and thought, "Why can't banking feel like this?"

Connection-Creating Ideas don't happen in a vacuum. They happen when you deliberately bring different worlds into contact with each other.

Your action steps:

Schedule one 'exploration hour' per week where you learn about
     something completely unrelated to your work
Keep an 'Inspiration File' of interesting approaches from other
     domains
When you see something clever in any context, ask: "How could
     we adapt this?"
Build relationships with people in different industries — they're
     your idea catalysts

*AI can analyze your industry data perfectly. But it will never sit
in a coffee shop, overhear a conversation about restaurant
loyalty programs, and think, "That could work for our customer
retention problem." That's uniquely human.
And it's trainable.*

Practice 3: The Customer Shadow

At least once a quarter, experience your product or service exactly
the way your customer does.

Not from your internal perspective. Not with your insider knowledge. Not with your special access or shortcuts. Like a complete
outsider.

If you work for a software company, create a new account and try
     to accomplish something without reading the documentation
     or asking anyone for help.
If you work in healthcare, try to schedule an appointment as
     a new patient.
If you work in financial services, try to open an account or file
     a claim.
If you work in manufacturing, follow your product from order
     to delivery as if you were the customer.

Pay attention to:

Where do you feel confused?
Where do you feel frustrated?
Where do you give up or settle for 'good enough'?
What takes way longer than it should?
What makes you feel stupid or incompetent (even though you're not)?
What makes you think, 'There has to be a better way'?

Those moments of friction? Those are where Customer-Obsessed Ideas live.

Reed Hastings felt the frustration of the late fee and imagined a better way. Jeff Bezos felt the frustration of driving to a bookstore only to find they didn't have the book he wanted, and imagined Amazon.

AI can tell you your Net Promoter Score. It can't feel what it's like to be your customer on a bad day. You can. If you practice.

HOW TO CHALLENGE THE PROCESS WITHOUT GETTING FIRED

Okay, so you're developing your idea muscle. You're asking opposite questions. You're cross-pollinating from other domains. You're shadowing the customer experience.

Ideas are flowing.

But here's the problem: Organizations don't like ideas. They SAY they do. They put innovation in the values statement. They hold brainstorming sessions. They talk about disrupting themselves before someone else does.

But when you actually show up with an idea that challenges how things are done? When you question sacred cows? When you suggest the opposite of the current strategy?

That's when you discover that organizations are designed to resist new ideas, not embrace them.

So how do you bring ideas forward without becoming the troublemaker who gets marginalized — or worse?

Here's what I've learned from watching people successfully challenge the process inside 34 Fortune 50 companies:

Rule 1: Start with Questions, Not Answers

Don't walk into a meeting and announce: "We're doing this wrong. Here's what we should do instead." That puts people on the defensive. It makes them protect the status quo. It makes you the enemy of everything they've built.

Instead, start with genuine questions:

"Help me understand why we [current approach]? I'm curious about the thinking behind it."
"What would happen if we tried [alternative]? What am I missing?"
"I noticed [interesting pattern]. Do you think that means anything?"
"What assumptions are we making that might be worth testing?"

Notice the difference? You're not attacking. You're exploring. You're inviting others into the thinking process.

Sometimes, your question will help people see an assumption they didn't know they were making. Sometimes, their answer will reveal why the current approach actually makes sense and your idea won't work. Either way, you learn and you don't make enemies.

*The best ideas don't come fully formed from one person.
They emerge through dialogue. Questions create dialogue.
Declarations create conflict.*

Rule 2: Bring Data, Even Imperfect Data

Ideas without evidence get dismissed as hunches. Ideas with evidence get consideration.

You don't need a full research study. You don't need statistical significance. You need something that suggests your idea might have merit:

Customer quotes: "I talked to five customers this week and three of them mentioned..."

Competitive intelligence: "I noticed three of our competitors are trying..."

Small experiments: "I tested this with my team for two weeks and here's what happened..."

Analogies: "This approach worked in [other industry] because..."

Basic numbers: "I ran the math and if we're right about this, the upside is..."

The manufacturing company that discovered customers cared about predictability over speed? That didn't come from a hunch. Someone ran a simple survey asking customers to rank what mattered most about delivery. The data contradicted the company's assumption. That made the idea credible.

You don't need perfect data. You need enough signal to suggest the current approach might be wrong and your idea might be right.

Rule 3: Propose an Experiment, Not a Revolution

Big ideas are scary. They require big commitments. They create big risks. They threaten people's careers if they fail.

So don't ask for a big commitment. Ask for a small experiment. Think big, start small.

Instead of: "We should completely change our pricing model."

Try: "What if we test this pricing approach with 50 customers for 30 days and see what happens?"

Instead of: "We need to rebuild our entire customer service operation."

Try: "What if one team tries the direct phone number approach for a quarter and we measure the results?"

Small experiments have magical properties:

They're low-risk, so decision-makers can say yes without fear
They generate real data, not hypothetical arguments
They create proof points that build support for bigger changes
They let you fail small instead of catastrophically
They give skeptics a chance to see results before committing

Netflix didn't launch with streaming in every country and bet the company on it. They started with DVD by mail. Then they tested streaming in limited markets. Then they expanded. Each small experiment proved the next bigger idea.

Your idea might be revolutionary.
Your proposal should be experimental.

Rule 4: Find an Executive Champion

Here's an uncomfortable truth: Great ideas from people without organizational power often go nowhere. The same idea from someone with executive sponsorship gets funded, resourced, and implemented.

It's not fair. But it's reality. So don't fight reality. Use it.

Before you propose your idea broadly, find an executive who has the power, the budget, and the political capital to back it. Share your thinking with them privately. Get their input. Refine the idea together.

Then when you propose it, you're not proposing alone. You have an executive champion who's bought in, who can run interference, who can mobilize resources, who can overcome organizational resistance.

How do you find that champion?

Look for executives who've supported innovation before
Identify who owns the problem your idea solves
Find someone who's expressed frustration with the status quo
Share your early thinking informally and watch for enthusiasm
Ask: "If I developed this idea more, would you want to hear about it?"

The credit union's direct phone number idea? It came from a mid-level manager. But she shared it with her VP first, got him excited, refined it together, and then they proposed it jointly to the CEO. With VP backing, the idea got a real hearing instead of being dismissed.

Your idea needs a champion. Find one before you need one.

WHEN YOUR IDEA GETS REJECTED (IT WILL)

Let's be honest: Most of your ideas will get rejected.

Not because they're bad. Not because you presented them wrong. Not because your organization is uniquely stupid.

Because that's the nature of ideas. Most don't work. Some are ahead of their time. Some solve the wrong problem. Some are right but the organization isn't ready.

So what do you do when your idea gets shot down?

Here's what NOT to do:

Don't take it personally and stop bringing ideas
Don't become bitter and cynical about the organization
Don't keep pushing the same idea over and over
Don't badmouth the decision-makers to colleagues
Don't externalize and blame others for not 'getting it'

Instead, do this — Learn from the rejection:

What legitimate concerns did people raise?
What evidence was I missing?
What was I wrong about?
What's a better version of this idea?
Is this the right idea for the wrong time?

Sometimes an idea gets rejected because it's not good. That's data. Learn from it and bring a better idea.

Sometimes an idea gets rejected because the organization isn't ready yet. That's also data. File it away and wait for the right moment.

Reed Hastings didn't invent streaming video in 1997 when he started Netflix. The technology wasn't ready. The market wasn't ready. He built DVD by mail first, proved the model, built the company, and THEN introduced streaming when the timing was right.

The best idea at the wrong time is just an early idea.
Be patient. Keep bringing ideas.
Eventually, timing and idea will align.

And here's the paradox: The very act of consistently bringing thoughtful, well-researched ideas — even ones that get rejected — builds your reputation as a strategic thinker. Over time, people start asking for your input. Your ideas get more consideration. You become the 'idea person' on your team.

That's the goal. Not getting every idea accepted. Becoming the person known for having ideas worth considering.

THE MYTH OF THE LONE GENIUS

Before we close this chapter, I need to bust one more myth about ideas: the myth of the lone genius.

We love stories about the brilliant individual who has the eureka moment in isolation. Steve Jobs inventing the iPhone. Reed Hastings imagining Netflix. The lone inventor in the garage.

It's a great story. It's also mostly fiction.

Every transformative idea is built on thousands of conversations, observations, failed experiments, and collaborative refinements.

Jobs didn't invent the smartphone. He synthesized existing technologies — touchscreens, mobile phones, music players, internet devices — and obsessed over making them work together elegantly. It took a team of hundreds.

Reed Hastings didn't work alone. He had co-founders, investors, engineers, customer feedback, market data. The idea evolved through countless iterations.

Great ideas are social. They're born in conversations. They're refined through feedback. They're improved through collaboration.

So don't try to develop your ideas alone. Share your early thinking with trusted colleagues. Ask for their honest feedback. Invite them to poke holes in your logic. Listen when they point out flaws.

Your ego wants your idea to be perfect before you share it. Your ego is wrong.

Your idea will get better through dialogue, not isolation.

FIND YOUR THINKING PARTNER

One of the most valuable things you can do for your career in the age of AI is to find a thinking partner — someone you can brainstorm with, someone who challenges your thinking, someone who makes your ideas better.

Not a cheerleader. Not someone who just agrees with everything you say. A real thinking partner who will tell you when your idea doesn't make sense, who will ask the hard questions, who will help you see blind spots.

This could be a colleague, a mentor, a friend in a different industry, even a spouse or partner who thinks differently than you do.

Schedule regular 'idea sessions' with your thinking partner. Share what you're working on. Explore opposite questions together. Cross-pollinate from your different experiences. Challenge each other's assumptions.

AI can be a tool in this process too. Use it to research, to analyze data, to play devil's advocate. But it's a tool, not a replacement for human dialogue.

The best ideas emerge from the intersection of different perspectives.
A single perspective is the enemy of reality.
Find someone whose perspective differs from yours and think together.

In 27 years inside Fortune 50 companies, I have noticed one consistent pattern among the professionals who became indispensable through disruption: they were never the lone geniuses. They were the connectors. They brought people together across silos. They translated ideas from one domain into language another domain could use. They made their organizations smarter by refusing to think alone.

You do not need to be the smartest person in the room. You need to be the person who makes the room smarter. That is a skill. And it starts with finding your thinking partner.

Oracle's recent restructuring illustrates this at scale. The company replaced 47 database administrators with three senior architects overseeing AI-automated systems. The three who remained were not the fastest at executing database tasks. They were the ones who understood how the systems were built, how they failed, and how to supervise them intelligently. They brought something the AI could not: the ability to imagine what the system was missing, to question what it was optimizing for, and to lead the humans working alongside it. In a world where AI executes brilliantly, the people who survive are not the best executors. They are the best thinkers. IDEAS is not a soft skill. It is survival infrastructure.

IDEAS: YOUR FIRST LAYER OF KRYPTONITE

Let's bring this home.

In a world where AI can execute brilliantly, where machines can optimize relentlessly, where automation can scale endlessly, your value as a human being comes from the one thing AI fundamentally can't do:

Imagine what doesn't exist yet

Challenge assumptions everyone else accepts
Connect ideas from different domains
Feel what customers feel and design for their delight

That's the power of IDEAS. That's your first ingredient of Kryptonite defense.

Build your idea muscle:

Practice the Daily Question Ritual — "What if we did the opposite?"
Schedule weekly Cross-Pollination time in a different domain
Shadow the customer experience at least once a quarter
Bring ideas forward strategically — questions, data, experiments, champions
Learn from rejections instead of being defeated by them
Find a thinking partner and think together

Do these things consistently and something remarkable happens: You become the person others come to for ideas. You become indispensable not because you can execute faster than AI — you can't — but because you can imagine possibilities AI can't see.

You become distinct.

Those prepared need not fear the forces at work.

But IDEAS alone aren't enough. You can have the best ideas in the world and still go extinct if you can't execute them faster than the market moves.

That's why the second ingredient of your Kryptonite defense is SPEED.

And that's where we're going next.

. . .

COMING UP IN CHAPTER 4:

In Chapter 4, we'll tackle the second ingredient of your Kryptonite defense: SPEED.

You'll discover why velocity matters more than perfection, how to make decisions faster without being reckless, and the surprising truth about why slow, deliberate organizations are becoming extinct faster than fast, imperfect ones.

Because in the age of AI, the race doesn't go to the strong or the smart. It goes to the fast.

And if you think you're already moving fast enough,
you're probably wrong.

CHAPTER 4:

SPEED

*The Second Ingredient
of Your Kryptonite Defense*

THE COMPANY THAT MOVED TOO SLOW

In 2007, Nokia was the undisputed king of mobile phones. They held 49.4% of the global market. They sold 435 million phones that year. Their brand was so dominant that in many countries, people didn't say 'mobile phone' — they said 'Nokia.'

Their leadership team was brilliant. Their engineers were world-class. Their supply chain was the envy of the industry. They had more money, more resources, more market knowledge than any competitor.

And then, on January 9, 2007, Steve Jobs walked onto a stage and introduced the iPhone.

Nokia's leadership watched the announcement. They analyzed the device. They ran the numbers. And they made a decision.

A careful decision. A deliberate decision.
A well-researched decision.

They decided the iPhone wasn't a significant threat.

Their reasoning was sound: No physical keyboard? Customers would hate it. No replaceable battery? Deal breaker. Expensive? Most people couldn't afford it. Locked to one carrier? Limited market. The touchscreen technology was impressive, but Nokia's engineers could match it. They just needed time to do it right.

So they formed committees. They commissioned studies. They developed strategic plans. They ran focus groups. They refined their approach.

They did everything a responsible, well-managed company should do.

THE NOKIA TIMELINE

January 2007: iPhone announced
June 2007: iPhone ships
2008: Nokia begins serious touchscreen development
2009: Strategic planning continues
2010: More refinement and testing
2011: Nokia's answer finally ships — four years later

By the time Nokia released their first credible touchscreen smartphone in 2011, the world had moved on. The App Store had created an ecosystem Nokia couldn't match. Customer expectations had shifted fundamentally. Competitors like Samsung had captured the Android market Nokia might have owned.

By the time Nokia shipped their answer, the question had changed.

Nokia's market share collapsed. By 2013, they sold their phone business to Microsoft for $7.2 billion — a fraction of what it had been worth just six years earlier.

What killed Nokia wasn't lack of resources. It wasn't lack of talent. It wasn't lack of market knowledge.

What killed Nokia was lack of speed.

They moved at the pace of traditional corporate decision-making: careful, deliberate, consensus-driven. Meanwhile, Apple moved at the pace of market disruption: fast, decisive, learning-by-doing.

Nokia optimized for being right. Apple optimized for being fast.

> *In a stable market, being right beats being fast.*
> *In a disrupted market, being fast beats being right.*

And we're living in a disrupted market — on steroids, with AI as the accelerant. No longer do the big eat the small. The fast eat the slow.

I have watched this dynamic accelerate dramatically in just the past 24 months. In a single week as I was completing this manuscript, 39 companies announced layoffs totaling more than 600,000 jobs driven by AI automation. The organizations moving at Nokia-speed on AI adoption are not just losing competitive advantage — they are accumulating a structural deficit that compounds daily. The organizations moving at Apple-speed are embedding AI into their workflows, retraining their teams, and locking in efficiencies their slow-moving competitors will spend years trying to replicate.

Speed in the age of AI is not a nice-to-have. It is the price of survival.

WHY SPEED BEATS PERFECTION IN THE AGE OF AI

Here's the uncomfortable truth that contradicts everything you were taught about quality and excellence:

> *In the age of AI and accelerating disruption, moving fast with 80% confidence beats moving slow with 95% confidence.*

This doesn't mean being reckless. It doesn't mean abandoning standards. It doesn't mean shipping garbage and hoping for the best.

It means fundamentally rethinking what 'good enough' means when the market is moving faster than your planning cycle.

Reason 1: The Market Moves Faster Than Your Planning Cycle

Look at Nokia's timeline again. Four years to respond to an existential threat. In stable times, that's reasonable. In disrupted times, that's fatal.

Because here's what else happened during those four years:

The App Store launched, creating an ecosystem advantage Nokia could never match

Millions of customers bought iPhones and invested in apps, creating switching costs

Developers learned iOS, making Android and iPhone the only platforms worth building for

Consumer expectations shifted, making physical keyboards feel obsolete

Competitors like Samsung moved fast, capturing the Android market Nokia might have owned

By the time Nokia shipped their answer, the question had changed.

This is the new reality: The time it takes you to thoroughly research, plan, and execute a perfect response is longer than the time it takes the market to make your response irrelevant.

So you have a choice: Move fast with good-enough solutions that you can iterate, or move slow with perfect solutions that arrive too late to matter.

Reason 2: Learning Beats Planning

Nokia's leaders spent years analyzing the iPhone, studying the market, planning their response. They gathered all the data, ran all the analyses, built all the models.

And they were still wrong about what customers wanted.

Meanwhile, Apple shipped the iPhone with significant flaws: No app store (initially), no 3G, no copy-paste, terrible battery life, frequent crashes. By any traditional quality standard, iPhone 1.0 was incomplete.

But Apple learned from real customers using real products in real situations. They learned what mattered — apps, speed, ecosystem — and what didn't — replaceable batteries, physical keyboards. They learned by shipping, measuring, and iterating.

By the time Nokia had analyzed their way to an answer,
Apple had learned their way to market dominance.

Here's a quote that has stayed with me for years:

"The light bulb did not come about by continuous
improvement of the candle."

Think about that. You could have perfected candle-making for centuries — made candles burn brighter, last longer, cost less. You'd never invent the light bulb. The light bulb required someone to imagine something completely different and move on it.

Nokia perfected mobile phones. Apple imperfectly seized the smartphone opportunity. Nokia's perfection lost to Apple's imperfect speed.

Real customer feedback from an imperfect product beats hypothetical feedback from a perfect plan. You can't predict how customers will actually use something until they use it. You can't know what features matter until you ship features and see which ones get used.

Speed gives you more learning cycles. More learning cycles give you better products. Better products give you market advantage.

Reason 3: AI Accelerates Everything, Including Your Competitors

Here's what's changed since Nokia's decline: AI doesn't just help you move faster. It helps everyone move faster. Your competitors. Your customers' expectations. The pace of market change.

Tasks that used to take weeks now take hours. Analyses that required teams now require prompts. Products that took months to develop now take weeks.

This creates a new equation:

If AI makes you 3x faster but makes your competitors 3x faster too, then anyone who was already faster than you just lapped you three times over.

The companies that were slow before AI are extinct after AI. The companies that were fast before AI are dominant after AI.

Speed isn't just an advantage anymore. It's table stakes. The minimum requirement to play the game.

Organizations that delayed meaningful AI adoption in 2023 and 2024 now face competitors carrying more than 18 months of embedded AI advantage — workflows redesigned, teams retrained, and efficiencies compounding daily. That gap does not close through planning. It closes only through speed.

And most organizations are structured for deliberation, not speed.

THE THREE SPEED TRAPS
(AND HOW TO AVOID THEM)

Okay, so speed matters. You get it. You're ready to move faster.

But here's the problem: Most attempts to 'move faster' fail spectacularly. They create chaos, burn out teams, ship garbage, and ultimately slow everything down even more.

Why? Because organizations fall into one of three speed traps.

Speed Trap 1: Confusing Urgency with Importance

I worked with a tech company where everyone was busy all the time. Meetings back-to-back. Emails at midnight. Everyone hustling. Everyone exhausted.

And nothing important was getting done.

The CEO kept saying 'We need to move faster!' So people moved faster — on everything. Every request was urgent. Every email needed immediate response. Every meeting was critical.

Speed without direction isn't speed. It's chaos.

The problem wasn't that they were moving too slow. The problem was they were moving fast on the wrong things.

Optimizing email response time instead of product development
Perfecting PowerPoint decks instead of shipping features
Having urgent meetings about meetings instead of making decisions

The Escape: Slow Down to Speed Up

Before you accelerate execution, get absolutely clear on what matters most. What are the three things that, if accomplished this quarter, would make everything else easier or irrelevant?

Then protect those three things from all the urgent-but-unimportant noise. Say no to good opportunities so you can say yes to great ones. Decline meetings that don't advance the critical three. Ignore emails that aren't mission-critical.

This is what I learned from working with Dr. Stephen Covey: You can't do everything fast. But you can do the right things fast and the wrong things not at all.

Most organizations try to do everything at 70% speed
and end up accomplishing nothing that matters.
High-performing organizations do three critical things at 100%
speed and politely decline everything else.

Speed Trap 2: Eliminating Decision-Making Process Instead of Improving It

I've watched companies try to speed up by eliminating their decision-making processes entirely.

"We need to move faster! No more committees! No more approval processes! Just do it!"

What happens? Chaos. Contradictory decisions. Resources wasted on initiatives that should never have been approved. Teams working at cross-purposes. Eventually, leadership reinstates all the processes — often making them even slower than before.

Here's the truth: The problem isn't that you have decision-making processes. The problem is that your processes were designed for a world that moved slower.

Traditional decision-making processes assume:
You have time to gather complete information
You can predict outcomes with reasonable accuracy
The cost of being wrong is higher than the cost of being slow
Consensus among stakeholders is achievable and valuable
The situation won't change significantly during the decision
    process

None of those assumptions hold true anymore.

So the answer isn't to eliminate process. It's to redesign process
for speed.

The Escape: The Fast Decision Framework

Not every decision deserves the same process. Categorize decisions into three types:

Type 1: Irreversible Decisions (*doors that lock behind you*)
Examples: Selling the company, shutting down a product line,
    hiring an executive
Process: Slow and careful — full analysis, broad input
Speed: Days to weeks, depending on complexity

Type 2: Reversible Decisions (*doors that can be reopened*)
Examples: Pricing changes, feature priorities, marketing cam-
    paigns, most hiring decisions
Process: Fast with feedback loops — 70% confidence threshold
Speed: Hours to days maximum

Type 3: Delegated Decisions (*let the people closest to the work decide*)
Examples: Implementation details, tactical choices, day-to-day
    operations
Process: None at senior level — trust the experts
Speed: Immediate

The problem with most organizations? They treat Type 2 and Type 3 decisions like Type 1 decisions. Everything requires the same careful, consensus-driven, extensively documented process.

Amazon has a rule: If a decision is reversible, it should take less than one day to make. Decide fast, ship it, learn from the results, adjust if needed. That's how you get speed without recklessness.

Speed Trap 3: Sacrificing Learning for Output

This is the most dangerous speed trap because it feels like success.

You're shipping fast. You're executing. You're hitting deadlines. Leadership is happy. Everyone feels productive.

And you're building the wrong thing at high speed.

I watched a software company ship five major features in six months. Impressive velocity. Their engineering team was cranking. Their product roadmap was getting checked off rapidly.

But they never paused to measure whether customers actually used the features they were shipping. After a year of impressive velocity, they looked at their usage data and discovered that three of the five major features had less than 5% adoption. Thousands of engineering hours building things customers didn't want.

Speed without learning is just fast failure.

The Escape: Build in Fast Feedback Loops

The companies that win don't just move fast. They learn fast. And learning requires feedback loops that are faster than your building cycles.

Ship small: Instead of one big release every quarter, ship small increments every week. Each increment teaches you something.

Measure immediately: Before you build the next thing, look at what happened with the last thing. Did anyone use it? Did it solve the problem? What surprised you?

Kill fast: If something isn't working, kill it immediately and redirect resources. Don't let sunk cost or pride keep you building the wrong thing.

Talk to customers continuously: Not surveys. Not focus groups. Real conversations with real customers about real usage. Weekly, not quarterly.

Make learning visible: Create a dashboard that shows what you're learning, not just what you're shipping. Celebrate insights, not just output.

The fastest companies aren't the ones that ship the most features.
They're the ones that learn the most per dollar spent
and time invested.

BUILDING YOUR PERSONAL SPEED MUSCLE

What you can change immediately is your personal speed. And here's what's powerful: When you become known as the person who moves fast, who makes decisions quickly, who ships results rapidly, you become indispensable.

Because in an age where everyone is drowning in information and paralyzed by options, the person who can cut through the noise and act decisively becomes incredibly valuable.

Before we dive into specific practices, understand this: Building personal speed requires developing agility — the ability to recognize realities quickly, pivot when needed, and maintain a 'what else can we do' mindset. Speed without agility is just frantic motion. You need:

Agility: The capacity to move quickly and change direction when circumstances demand it

Reality Recognition: The ability to see situations as they are, not as you wish they were

Flexibility: The willingness to adapt your approach when the first approach isn't working

Drive: The determination to keep moving even when the path isn't clear

Change Embrace: The mindset that treats change as opportunity, not threat

These aren't separate from speed — they're what make speed sustainable.

Practice 1: The Two-Hour Rule

Any request that requires less than two hours of work gets done the day it's received.

No 'I'll get to it later.' No 'Let me think about it.' No adding it to next week's to-do list.

If it takes less than two hours, it gets done today.

Why? Because the mental overhead of tracking open items, the context-switching cost of revisiting them later, and the opportunity cost of delayed action almost always exceeds the two hours you'd save by batching them.

Plus, you build a reputation as someone who gets things done fast. When your colleagues know you'll respond quickly, they come to you first. That makes you more valuable, more visible, and more indispensable.

Examples of two-hour tasks:

Responding to important emails
Reviewing a document and providing feedback
Making a simple decision on something waiting for your input
Having a quick call to resolve something
Creating a first draft (doesn't have to be perfect)
Fixing a small bug or issue

The Two-Hour Rule doesn't mean saying yes to everything. It means quickly handling or deciding on everything that doesn't require deep work. If something requires more than two hours, schedule it properly. But most things don't require more than two hours. They just sit on lists for days because we treat everything the same.

Fast people know the difference. They knock out the quick stuff immediately, which frees up mental space and time for the deep work that actually requires it.

Practice 2: The 70% Decision Threshold

Most people wait until they're 90-95% certain before making a decision. That certainty comes from more research, more analysis, more input, more validation.

And by the time they're 95% certain, the opportunity has passed or the situation has changed.

Here's what I learned from working with fast-moving Fortune 50 companies: The best decision-makers operate at 70% confidence. When they're 70% sure they know the right answer, they decide and move forward.

But here's the key: They build in fast feedback mechanisms so they can course-correct if the 30% uncertainty reveals problems.

Think of it like driving in fog. You can't see the whole road. But you can see well enough to move forward cautiously — and you adjust as you get more information.

How to implement the 70% threshold:

Set a deadline for decisions: 'I will decide on this by end of day Friday.' The deadline forces you to work with available information.

Ask: 'What's the cost of waiting?' Often the cost of delay exceeds the cost of being wrong.

Ask: 'Can this be reversed?' If yes, the bar for certainty should be lower.

Decide, then monitor closely: Make the decision at 70%, but pay extra attention to early signals.

Document your reasoning: Write down why you made the decision so you can learn from it later.

The 70% rule doesn't apply to everything. Type 1 decisions — the truly irreversible ones — might need 90% confidence or higher. But most decisions aren't Type 1. Most are reversible, adjustable, course-correctable.

For reversible decisions, waiting for 95% certainty just means someone else makes the decision by moving faster.

Practice 3: The Bias Toward Action

When faced with a choice between acting and waiting for more information, bias toward action.

This doesn't mean being reckless. It means defaulting to 'let's try something and learn' rather than 'let's study it more.'

I worked with a product team that spent six months debating the best approach to a customer problem. They had meetings.

They created frameworks. They compared options. They modeled outcomes.

Finally, I asked: 'What's the simplest version of solution A that we could ship next week?'

They looked at me like I was crazy. 'Next week? We haven't finalized the approach!'

"Exactly. Ship something small next week. Learn from what happens. Use that learning to make the next decision. You'll know more from one week of customer feedback than six months of internal debate."

They shipped a basic version the following week. Customers loved parts of it and hated other parts. That real feedback settled the six-month debate in one week.

Action generates information. Waiting generates anxiety.

How to build your bias toward action:

In meetings, always ask: 'What's the smallest thing we could try this week?'

When you're uncertain, propose an experiment instead of more analysis

When someone says 'We need to study this more,' ask 'What would we learn from studying that we won't learn from trying?'

Keep a 'bias toward action' scorecard: track how many times you act versus wait

Celebrate fast failures as learning opportunities, not mistakes

Here is what I have seen in 27 years of working inside organizations of every size and type: the most dangerous pattern is not recklessness. It is the slow drift of incremental caution. Leaders take one bold step, then pause to let everyone catch up, then take a few small steps, then wait for consensus, then study the results, then form a committee. Each pause feels reasonable in isolation. Together, they add up to paralysis dressed as prudence.

In a world moving at the pace of AI-driven disruption, incremental change is not a safe middle path. It is a slower path to the same destination as standing still. The forces at work do not reward careful. They reward committed. When you believe something is right, act on it fully. If it works, build on it fast. If it does not, cut your losses, extract the learning, and move again. What you cannot afford is the prolonged, hedged, half-committed approach that satisfies no one and accomplishes nothing.

The people who win in the age of AI aren't the ones who make perfect decisions. They're the ones who make good decisions fast and course-correct faster.

BUT WHAT ABOUT QUALITY?

I know what some of you are thinking: 'This all sounds great, but what about quality? What about excellence? What about not shipping garbage?'

Fair question. Let me be direct:

Speed and quality aren't opposites. They're partners. But we have to redefine what quality means in a fast-moving environment.

OLD DEFINITION OF QUALITY:

Everything is polished before it ships
No bugs, no rough edges, no imperfections
Fully featured, complete, finished

Validated through extensive testing
Perfect on delivery day

NEW DEFINITION OF QUALITY:

Core functionality works reliably
Solves the customer's primary problem
Can be improved based on real usage
Shipped fast enough to matter
Gets better over time through iteration

The iPhone 1.0 wasn't 'quality' by the old definition. It was missing obvious features, it crashed regularly, the battery life was terrible.

But it was quality by the new definition. It solved the core problem — internet in your pocket with a beautiful interface — it could be improved through software updates, and it shipped when it mattered.

Nokia's eventual touchscreen phones were 'quality' by the old definition. Polished, tested, feature-complete. But they failed the new definition: they shipped too late to matter.

Quality = Core Problem Solved × Speed to Market × Ability to Iterate

A solution that's 80% complete but ships when customers need it and can be improved beats a solution that's 100% complete but ships too late to matter.

Speed with quality builds on itself. Slow with quality just arrives late.

BUILDING A CULTURE OF SPEED

Individual speed matters. But organizational speed requires culture.

You can be the fastest person on your team, but if you're embedded in a slow organization, you'll get frustrated or you'll slow down to match.

Here are the five cultural shifts that create speed:

1. Celebrate Fast Decisions, Not Just Right Decisions

In slow cultures, people get praised for being right. So everyone waits to be certain before deciding.

In fast cultures, people get praised for deciding quickly AND learning fast from the results.

Instead of asking "Did you make the right call?" ask "How fast did you decide, and what did you learn?"

*When people know they won't be punished for fast decisions
that turn out wrong, they stop waiting
for perfect information.*

2. Make 'Waiting' Visible and Expensive

In most organizations, action is visible. Waiting is invisible. You can see when someone ships something. You can't see when someone is sitting on a decision.

Make waiting visible:
Track average time-to-decision for your team and make it public
In status meetings, ask: 'What's waiting on a decision?' not just
  'What got done?'

Calculate and share the opportunity cost of delayed decisions
Celebrate when someone makes a fast decision, even if it's not perfect

*When waiting becomes visible and expensive,
people start moving faster.*

3. Shrink the Approval List

Every person on an approval chain slows things down. Not because they're bad people, but because they have other priorities, limited time, and their own need to be certain before approving.

Fast organizations ruthlessly shrink approval lists:
Default to single-approver for most decisions
For decisions requiring multiple approvers, require response
     within 24 hours or approval is automatic
Push decisions down to the lowest level possible
Replace 'approval' with 'notification' for reversible decisions

*Amazon has a rule: Any decision that requires more than two
approvers should be questioned. Either it's big enough for executive
involvement — or it's small enough that the person closest to the
work should just decide.*

4. Reward Learning Over Perfection

In performance reviews, in team meetings, in all-hands presentations, celebrate the teams that learned the most — not just the teams that executed flawlessly.

Ask:
What did we learn this quarter that changed our strategy?
What experiment failed but taught us something valuable?
What assumption did we discover was wrong?
How fast did we pivot when we got new information?

When you reward learning, people move faster because they're not afraid to be wrong. They're excited to discover what works.

5. Model Speed From the Top

Culture flows downhill. If leadership is slow, the organization will be slow. If you're a leader, you set the pace:

Return emails within 24 hours (or set an auto-response with next steps)

Make decisions in meetings, not after meetings

Approve or reject proposals within 48 hours

When you can't decide fast, explain why and set a clear decision deadline

Visibly kill projects that aren't working instead of letting them linger

Your team watches what you do, not what you say. If you move fast, they'll move fast. If you're cautious and slow, they'll be cautious and slow.

The data on this is compelling. Cisco's internal People Intelligence research found that employees whose direct leaders actively use AI tools are twice as likely to adopt AI themselves. The reverse is equally true: when leaders wait, their teams wait. Leadership behavior on speed and adoption does not stay at the top of the organization. It cascades through every layer below it.

Speed is contagious. So is slowness. Choose wisely.

SPEED: YOUR SECOND LAYER OF KRYPTONITE

Let's bring this home.

You can have the best ideas in the world. You can imagine possibilities no one else sees. You can challenge assumptions brilliantly.

*But if you're slow, someone else will execute your ideas
before you do.*

Speed isn't about being reckless. It's about moving fast enough that you can learn and adapt before the market moves on. It's about making good decisions quickly instead of perfect decisions slowly. It's about shipping 80% solutions that you can improve instead of 100% solutions that arrive too late.

Remember:
The market moves faster than your planning cycle
Learning beats planning
AI accelerates everything, including your competitors
Quality means 'solves the problem and ships when it matters,' not 'perfect on day one'
Speed is a muscle you can build — both personally and organizationally

Nokia had better resources than Apple. More market knowledge, more engineers, more money.

But Apple moved faster. And in a disrupted market, fast beats big every single time.

Those prepared need not fear the forces at work.

You've now got two ingredients of your Kryptonite defense: IDEAS and SPEED.

But ideas and speed aren't enough if you don't have the right TALENT around you — and if you're not developing yourself into someone who can't be replaced by a machine.

That's where we're going next.

. . .

COMING UP IN CHAPTER 5:

In Chapter 5, we'll tackle the third ingredient of your Kryptonite defense: TALENT.

You'll discover why the people around you matter more than ever, how to become someone others want to work with, and the critical difference between being skilled and being valuable in the age of AI.

Because here's the truth: AI can match your technical skills.
But it can't match the power of the right people,
working together, toward something that matters.
That's your sustainable advantage — if you know how to use it.

TALENT

*The Third Ingredient
of Your Kryptonite Defense*

THE ENGINEER WHO COULD DO EVERYTHING, EXCEPT KEEP A JOB

In 2019, I got a call from a VP of Engineering at a major tech company. She had a problem.

"We just let go of one of the most technically brilliant engineers I've ever worked with," she said. "And I need you to help me understand why we had to do it."

The engineer — let's call him David — had a resume that would make any recruiter salivate. MIT graduate. Published research. Patents. Expert in machine learning, systems architecture, cloud infrastructure. He could code in twelve languages. He could debug systems that made other engineers weep.

By any technical measure, David was exceptional.

So why did they fire him?

"Because he was brilliant alone and useless on a team."

She told me the story: David would take on complex projects and solve them elegantly. But he wouldn't communicate his approach. He wouldn't share his code reviews. He wouldn't mentor junior engineers. When others asked questions, he'd get visibly annoyed at having to explain 'obvious' things.

He missed deadlines because he insisted on perfect solutions instead of good-enough solutions that the team could iterate on. He refused to use the team's established patterns because his way was 'better.' He created technical debt because nobody else could understand or maintain his code.

Worst of all, he made other talented engineers want to leave. Two quit specifically citing David as the reason.

"The breaking point," the VP said, "was when I realized we were more productive without him than with him. His technical brilliance was outweighed by the friction he created."

She paused, then added something that has stayed with me:

"In five years, AI will be able to do most of what David does technically. But AI will never be able to do what our best engineers do — collaborate, communicate, elevate others, and solve problems together that no individual could solve alone."

That's the paradox of talent in the age of AI: The technical skills that got you hired are becoming table stakes. The collaboration skills that make you valuable are becoming irreplaceable.

I have been making this argument for 27 years — long before AI made it urgent. Inside Intel, Apple, PepsiCo, Caterpillar, and dozens of other Fortune 50 companies, the pattern has always been the same: the people who get promoted, protected during cuts, and asked to lead transformation initiatives are never simply the most technically capable. They are the ones who make everyone around them better. AI has not changed that pattern. It has just made the penalty for ignoring it more severe and more swift.

Jensen Huang, the CEO of NVIDIA — the company whose technology powers virtually every major AI system on Earth — was asked to define intelligence. His answer should stop every professional in their tracks. He said the old definition of smart, the person who is technically brilliant and solves complex problems, is a commodity. "Everybody thought software programming was the ultimate smart profession," Huang said. "Look what is the first thing AI is solving. Software programming." Then he offered his own definition: "My definition of smart is someone who sits at the intersection of being technically astute but has human empathy. The ability to infer the unspoken. The unknowable." He called it seeing around corners. The ability to sense when something is wrong before anyone can prove it, to feel what the data cannot yet show, to make a judgment call when the algorithm has no answer. That person, Huang added, might score horribly on the SAT. The man running a trillion-dollar company that is reshaping every industry on the planet just told you that technical brilliance is being commoditized and human judgment is the last scarce resource. That is not a theory. That is a market signal from the most important infrastructure company in the age of AI.

Jensen Huang, the CEO of NVIDIA — the company whose chips power virtually every major AI system on Earth — was recently asked a simple question: who is the smartest person you have ever met? He did not name a scientist or a billionaire. Instead, he dismantled the entire concept of what smart means. "The definition of smart," he said, "is somebody who's intelligent, solves technical problems. But I find that's a commodity." He went further: "Everybody thought software programming was the ultimate smart profession. Look what is the first thing AI is solving." Then he offered his own definition. "My definition of smart is someone who sits at the intersection of being technically astute but has human empathy. The ability to infer the unspoken. The unknowable." He called it seeing around corners. The ability to sense a problem before it shows up on a dashboard, to feel when something is wrong before anyone can prove it. And then came the line that should stop every hiring manager, every leader, and every professional in their tracks: "That person might actually score horribly on the SAT." The man running a trillion-dollar company just told you that when intelligence becomes as cheap as electricity, the only thing that stays scarce is human judgment. That is not a theory. That is the operating philosophy of the most important technology company on the planet. And it is the entire argument of this chapter.

WHY TECHNICAL SKILLS ARE NECESSARY BUT NOT SUFFICIENT

Let me be clear about something: Technical skills matter. Being good at your craft matters. Expertise matters.

If you're a terrible engineer, it doesn't matter how well you collaborate. If you're a mediocre salesperson, your people skills won't compensate. If you don't know your domain, no amount of emotional intelligence will save you.

This chapter is NOT about replacing technical excellence with soft skills. It's about understanding that technical excellence is the entry fee — it gets you in the game, but it doesn't keep you in the game anymore.

THE GREAT AI SKILL REPLICATION

AI is getting exponentially better at replicating technical skills.

It can write code. Debug systems. Analyze data. Create financial models. Draft legal documents. Design marketing campaigns. Generate architectural plans. Process insurance claims.

In 2024, GitHub Copilot writes 46% of the code in projects where it's enabled. That percentage is climbing every month. AI can pass the bar exam. It can pass medical licensing exams. It can solve complex mathematical proofs. It can create designs that win awards.

And yet the most revealing data point is not about what AI can do technically. It is about what humans do when they work alongside it. Cisco's internal People Intelligence research found that employees whose direct leaders actively use AI tools are twice as likely to adopt AI themselves. The difference was not access — every employee had the same tools. The difference was human behavior at the leadership level.

That single finding illustrates what this chapter is fundamentally about: in the age of AI, your human skills — how you lead, how you model, how you influence — matter more than ever. Technical capability gets you in the room. How you show up determines whether you stay.

Here's what AI can't replicate:
The ability to read a room and know when the team is burned out
The judgment to know which technical approach will get team buy-in
The communication skill to explain complex ideas to non-technical stakeholders
The empathy to mentor a struggling junior team member
The trust built over time that makes people want to work with you
The credibility that makes your recommendations get implemented
The collaboration that makes $1 + 1 = 5$ instead of 2

David had none of these. And that's why his extraordinary technical skills couldn't save him.

The future doesn't belong to the most technically skilled individuals. It belongs to technically skilled people who can work with other technically skilled people to accomplish things no individual — and no AI — could accomplish alone.

BECOMING A T-SHAPED PROFESSIONAL IN THE AGE OF AI

There's a concept in talent development called the T-shaped professional.

The vertical part of the T represents deep expertise in one domain. The horizontal part represents broad skills across multiple domains.

In the pre-AI world, being I-shaped — deep expertise, narrow breadth — could work. You could specialize so deeply that your expertise alone made you valuable.

In the AI world, I-shaped professionals are endangered. Because AI can replicate depth better than it can replicate breadth — especially the human breadth of collaboration, communication, and contextual judgment.

THE T-SHAPED TALENT MODEL

VERTICAL BAR (DEEP EXPERTISE — AI IS COMING FOR THIS):

Technical mastery in your domain
Subject matter expertise that takes years to develop
Problem-solving capability in your specialty
Ability to handle complex challenges in your field

HORIZONTAL BAR (HUMAN SKILLS — YOUR DURABLE ADVANTAGE):

Communication: Translating expertise for different audiences
Collaboration: Working effectively across teams and disciplines
Emotional Intelligence: Reading situations and people
Influence: Getting ideas adopted and implemented
Mentorship: Developing others and sharing knowledge
Judgment: Knowing when to use which approach
Adaptability: Pivoting when circumstances change

AI is coming for the vertical bar. It's getting better at technical tasks every day. But the horizontal bar? That's where humans maintain durable advantage.

David was all vertical bar. Incredible depth, zero breadth. And that made him replaceable — ironically, by both AI and by less brilliant engineers who could work well with others.

THE ENGINEER WHO MADE HERSELF INDISPENSABLE

Let me tell you about Maya, who worked on the same team as David before he was let go.

Maya was a good engineer. Not brilliant like David. She didn't have patents. She wasn't publishing research. She was solidly competent — maybe 80th percentile technically.

But here's what Maya did that David didn't:

When a junior engineer got stuck, Maya would take 30 minutes to walk them through the problem. Not just give them the answer — teach them how to think through it. She built a reputation as the person who made others better.

When the product team had questions about technical feasibility, Maya could explain complex trade-offs in language they understood. She became the bridge between engineering and product.

When the team was drowning in technical debt, Maya didn't just complain about it. She created a proposal showing the business impact of the debt, the cost of fixing it, and a phased approach that balanced new features with tech debt reduction. Leadership approved it because she spoke their language.

When disagreements arose about technical approach, Maya facilitated the discussion instead of forcing her view. She'd say, "Let's list out the pros and cons of each approach, then decide based on our priorities." Teams made better decisions because of her facilitation.

Today, Maya is a principal engineer and leads a team of 15. Not because she's the most technically brilliant person in the company. Because she makes everyone around her better.

"When I think about who I can't afford to lose, Maya is at the top of the list. Not because of what she builds, but because of who she develops and how she elevates everyone."

THE CHOICE: BE DAVID OR BE MAYA

You have a choice in your career.

You can be David: Technically brilliant, individually productive, and ultimately replaceable by either AI or by someone less skilled who plays better with others.

Or you can be Maya: Technically solid, exponentially more valuable because of how you multiply the effectiveness of everyone around you, and irreplaceable because your value transcends any individual task.

Organizations will always keep the Mayas and let go of the Davids — even when the Davids are more technically skilled. Why?

Maya builds organizational capability. David builds individual output.
Maya makes the team better. David makes the team dependent or frustrated.
Maya's impact compounds. David's impact is linear.
Maya's value grows as AI handles more technical tasks. David competes with AI.
Maya attracts talent. David repels it.

The irony? David probably thinks he's more valuable because he's more technically skilled. He doesn't understand that technical skill is becoming less scarce while human skills that amplify teams are becoming more scarce.

The question isn't whether you're technically good. The question is: Are you someone people want to work with? Are you someone who makes others better? Are you building capability beyond yourself?

That's what TALENT means in the age of AI.

THE FIVE WAYS TO BUILD YOUR TALENT VALUE

Here are five practices that build your talent value in the age of AI:

1. Become a Multiplier, Not Just a Contributor

A contributor adds their own output. A multiplier amplifies others' output.

Contributors think: "How much can I personally accomplish?"

Multipliers think: "How can I help everyone accomplish more?"

Here's what this looks like in practice:

Share your knowledge proactively. Document your processes. Create guides that help others do what you do.

When you solve a hard problem, don't just solve it. Explain your thinking process so others learn to solve similar problems.

Look for bottlenecks in the team and remove them. If everyone is waiting on you for reviews, create a review process that works without you.

Ask: "Who else should know this?" and bring them into the conversation.

Measure your success not just by what you deliver, but by how much capability you build in others.

I worked with a data scientist who built a reputation as a multiplier. Whenever she created a new analysis model, she'd record a video explaining her approach, the tools she used, the trade-offs she considered. She built a library of these videos. Within a year, her team could handle analyses she used to be the only one capable of doing.

Did that make her less valuable? No. It made her extraordinarily valuable because leadership could trust her with bigger, more strategic problems knowing she'd build capability, not just deliver output.

She got promoted to director not because she was the best analyst, but because she made everyone better analysts.

2. Master the Art of Translation

One of the most valuable skills in any organization is the ability to translate between different domains.

Translating technical concepts to business stakeholders. Translating business needs to technical teams. Translating strategy to tactics. Translating customer problems to product requirements.

AI can't do this well because effective translation requires understanding context, audience, and unspoken concerns that vary by situation.

Here's how to build translation skills:

Before explaining anything, ask yourself: What does this audience care about? What keeps them up at night? What language do they speak?

Practice the 3-level explanation: Explain your work to an expert in your field, a smart person in a different field, and a 12-year-old. All three should understand the core idea.

Use analogies from their world, not yours. If you're talking to sales, use sales analogies. If you're talking to finance, speak in ROI.

Listen for confusion and adjust in real-time. If eyes glaze over, stop and say: "Let me try explaining that differently."

Strip out jargon ruthlessly. Every piece of domain-specific terminology is a barrier to understanding.

Maya once explained a complex architecture decision to the executive team this way: "Think of our current system like a building with plumbing from 1950. It still works, but when something breaks, parts are hard to find and fixes take forever. The new architecture is like modern plumbing — easier to maintain, more reliable, and ready for future needs. The remodel costs $2M but saves us $500K per year in maintenance and reduces customer-impacting outages by 80%."

The executives understood immediately. They approved the budget. The technical details didn't matter to them — the business impact did. Maya spoke their language.

3. Build Trust Through Reliability

Here's something most people miss: Your talent isn't just about what you can do. It's about whether people believe you'll actually do it.

Trust is built through consistent reliability. Do what you say you'll do, when you say you'll do it, the way you said you'd do it.

This sounds basic. It's not. Most people are terrible at this. They overpromise and underdeliver. They miss deadlines without communication. They say yes to things they can't actually do.

Here's what reliability looks like:

Underpromise and overdeliver. If something will take 3 days, say 4 days and deliver in 3.

If you're going to miss a deadline, communicate early with options. Don't wait until the deadline passes.

Keep commitments visible. Use systems that make your commitments transparent so nothing falls through cracks.

Say no to things you can't actually deliver well. Better to decline than to accept and fail.

When you make a mistake — and you will — own it immediately, fix it, and learn from it. Don't make the same mistake twice.

Maya became someone people could bet on. When she said she'd do something, it happened. This built a currency of trust that made everything else easier. People wanted her on projects. Leadership gave her opportunities. Teams fought to work with her.

David, for all his brilliance, was unreliable. He'd disappear into his work and miss meetings. He'd blow deadlines pursuing perfect solutions. People couldn't count on him, so they didn't want to work with him.

4. Develop Judgment, Not Just Skills

Skills are about knowing how to do something. Judgment is about knowing when to do it — and when not to.

AI has skills. It doesn't have judgment.

Judgment is knowing:

When to push for perfection and when good enough is actually good enough
When to follow process and when to break it
When to escalate and when to handle it yourself
When to move fast and when to slow down
When to be direct and when to be diplomatic
When the team needs encouragement and when they need tough feedback

You can't learn judgment from a book or a training program. You develop it through experience, reflection, and learning from mistakes. Here's how to accelerate:

After every significant decision, ask: What did I get right? What did I get wrong? What would I do differently?
Find mentors with good judgment and watch how they think through situations.
Before making a decision, pause and ask: "What am I optimizing for here?"
Seek feedback on your judgment, not just your execution. Ask: "Was my call on that situation right? What did I miss?"

People with good judgment become trusted advisors.
They're the ones leaders come to for counsel. That's a form
of value AI will never replace.

• • •

THE ACCOUNTABILITY FOUNDATION OF TALENT

There is one human capability that sits underneath every other talent discussed in this chapter, and it is the one most professionals underinvest in because it is the most uncomfortable to develop.

Accountability.

Not the organizational version of accountability, the performance reviews and consequence management that most companies call accountability but is really compliance. The personal version. The kind that starts with you, before anyone is watching, before anyone requires it.

Here is what makes genuine accountability so rare, and so powerful, it is a choice. Nobody can make anybody accountable. You can hold people accountable in a positive, principled manner. But you cannot make someone accountable. Accountability is a personal decision, to rise above your circumstances and take the ownership necessary to achieve the results that matter most to you.

ABOVE AND BELOW THE WATER

The most useful framework I have ever used for understanding accountability culture is an image I have shared with audiences around the globe for 27 years. Picture a pool of water.

'Above the water,' you are focused on what you can control. You are like an engine propelling your team and organization forward. You are engaged, resolute, driven, persevering, looking for solutions around every obstacle. The question running through your mind is, what else can I do to get the result that matters most to me, my team, or my organization? That is the Solve It question. That is what I refer to as, 'above-the-water thinking.'

'Below the water,' everything looks different. You are focused on what you cannot control. You are like an anchor holding the organization back. The primary thinking below the water is this, it is not my fault, and there is nothing I can do about it. Blame. Excuses. Bitterness. Cynicism. Entitlement. Disengagement. Frozen in place while the world moves forward without you.

Let me give you two examples that have stayed with me for decades.

In the early 1990s, Jack in the Box had an E. coli outbreak in their hamburger meat. Four children died. Hundreds became seriously ill. Some had to have organ transplants. Their immediate response was to blame the supermarket where they sourced the meat. The supermarket blamed the meat packers. The meat packers blamed the USDA. The USDA blamed Congress. The blame game went on and on. How long did it take Jack in the Box to recover financially? Seven years. They still do not exist on the East Coast.

Compare that to Johnson and Johnson and Tylenol in the late 1980s. A criminal laced capsules with cyanide. Seven people died. Tylenol had 38 percent market share at the time. Their immediate response was to pull every bottle from every shelf nationwide and incinerate 300 million dollars worth of product. Their market share went from 38 percent to zero in 48 hours. Then they invented tamper-proof packaging. How long did it take them to recover their 38 percent market share? Two months.

Here is the part of that story that matters most: most people would have given Tylenol a pass. It was not their fault. Some lunatic did this. But that was not their thinking. Their mindset was: it was our fault. We did not do enough to protect the consumer. That above-the-water ownership is what made the difference.

Every single one of us, at some point, will be put in a situation where we could, if we wanted to, blame someone else for putting us there. And every moment you spend below the water playing the blame game is a moment you are not doing the one thing that actually matters most, finding a solution.

There is almost a gravitational force that pulls people below the water. It is not wrong to go there sometimes. Sometimes you need to blow off steam, figure out the reasons, learn from what happened. It can be therapeutic. What would be wrong is staying there. To have your mail forwarded below the water. To live your life anchored in blame while everyone around you is moving forward. We all know people like that.

THE 4 KEYS TO ACCOUNTABILITY

When someone chooses to rise above the water, they move through four keys, a sequence of thinking and action that separates professionals who are genuinely accountable from those who perform accountability while privately externalizing everything.

The first key is Recognize Realities. Accountable professionals see their situation clearly, including the parts that are inconvenient. They do not filter information through the lens of what they want to be true. They do not wait for someone else to name the problem. They practice open and candid communication, they stay open to others' perspectives, they ask for and offer feedback, they talk about the elephants in the room, and they anticipate opportunities rather than react to threats.

The second key is Accept Ownership. Seeing a problem is not the same as owning it. Ownership means accepting full responsibility for your contribution to the situation. Not partial responsibility. Not shared responsibility contingent on what others did. Your part. Fully. Without deflection. Can you be partially accountable? No. Partial accountability is just a slower form of not being accountable.

The third key is Create Solutions. Ownership without action is just guilt. This is the Solve It question in practice, what else can I do to get the result I want? Not who should have prevented this. Not whose fault was it. What can I do, right now, to move forward? If you truly own a result, if you really want it, there is always some step you can take to get closer to it. Always.

The fourth key is Exercise Action. Creating a solution in your head is not a solution. Accountable professionals execute on their commitments. They do what they said they would do, when they said they would do it, at the level of quality they committed to. Consistently. You cannot drive from Pittsburgh to New York and stop in Kansas and say you arrived. You have to complete the entire journey. Accountability is the same. It is a process, and you must move through the entire process.

These four keys are not a personality type. They are a practice. They can be developed at any level, in any role, regardless of title or authority. And it is not about how skillfully you execute each key. It is about frequency. The more often your team displays these behaviors, the more likely they are to achieve and exceed whatever results they are working toward. The results your team must achieve in order to help you continue to thrive and grow.

As you assess your TALENT score on the Kryptonite Scorecard, Behavior 18 asks whether you hold yourself accountable for outcomes and take ownership regardless of formal authority. That behavior is the visible tip of the pool. The question underneath it, the one that determines your score honestly, is: do you live above the water or below it?

. . .

5. Be Someone People Want to Work With

This is the simplest and most important practice: Be pleasant to work with.

Sounds basic, right? Yet this is where so many talented people — like David — fail.

Being pleasant to work with doesn't mean being a pushover. It doesn't mean avoiding conflict or tough conversations. It doesn't mean sacrificing standards.

It means:

Treating people with respect even when you disagree
Assuming positive intent until proven otherwise
Giving credit generously and accepting blame willingly
Making others feel heard and valued
Managing your emotions instead of dumping them on others
Being willing to help even when it's not your job
Celebrating others' wins without jealousy
Admitting when you're wrong without defensiveness

Here's the reality: When opportunities arise, managers give them to people they enjoy working with. When cuts happen, managers keep people they want around. When teams form, people choose teammates they trust and like.

Two people with equal technical skills? The one who's pleasant to work with gets the promotion, the opportunity, the resources. It's not purely meritocratic — but it's human nature, and it's not changing.

DRAWING OUT TALENT IN OTHERS: THE MULTIPLIER'S SECRET

So far we've talked about building your own talent value. But here's what separates good professionals from indispensable ones:

The ability to draw out talent in everyone around you — regardless of whether you have any formal authority over them.

Maya didn't just become valuable because of her own skills. She became indispensable because she made everyone around her better. She drew out capabilities in junior engineers they didn't know they had. She created an environment where people voluntarily gave discretionary effort.

UNDERSTANDING HOW PEOPLE DEVELOP (OR DON'T)

Before you can draw out talent in others, you need to understand how talent actually develops. And it's not what most people think.

Most managers try to develop people by telling them what to do. Instructions, directions, policies, procedures. When that doesn't work, they tell them again — louder this time.

But that's not how people develop. Here's how people actually develop:

THE RESULTS MODEL

EXPERIENCES → BELIEFS → ACTIONS → RESULTS

Every experience you have creates a belief. That belief drives your actions. Your actions produce your results.

Here's why this matters: If you want someone to take different actions, you can't just tell them to take different actions. You have to change their beliefs. And to change their beliefs, you have to create new experiences.

Example: You have a team member who never speaks up in meetings. You tell them, 'You need to contribute more.' Nothing changes. Why?

Because their belief is: 'When I speak up, I get shot down' or 'My ideas aren't valuable' or 'It's safer to stay quiet.' That belief came from experiences. Maybe they shared an idea once and got criticized. Maybe they watched others get dismissed.

Telling them to speak up doesn't change the belief. You have to create NEW experiences that develop a NEW belief. So instead, you:

Ask them directly for their input in meetings
When they share something, build on it publicly and give credit
Give them smaller, safer opportunities to contribute first
Acknowledge their contributions afterward — privately and publicly

Over time, these new experiences create a new belief. That new belief drives new action. This is how you draw out talent — not by telling people what to do, but by creating experiences that develop beliefs that drive the actions you want to see.

And remember: Every action YOU take is an experience for everyone watching you.

When you snap at someone in a meeting — what belief does that create?
When you publicly credit someone's contribution — what belief does that create?
When you admit you were wrong — what belief does that create?

You are ALWAYS creating experiences. The question is: Are those experiences developing the beliefs you want people to have?

THE DISCRETIONARY PERFORMANCE ZONE

Here's a question: What percentage of their capability do most people bring to work?

Research suggests that most employees operate at about 40-60% of their actual capability. The rest sits in what we call the Discretionary Performance Zone.

The Discretionary Performance Zone is the gap between what someone HAS to do to keep their job and what they COULD do if they were fully engaged.

THE THREE PERFORMANCE LEVELS

MINIMUM ACCEPTABLE PERFORMANCE: What you have to do to not get fired. This is the floor.

EXPECTED PERFORMANCE: What's outlined in your job description. This is what most people deliver.

DISCRETIONARY PERFORMANCE: What you could do if you chose to go above and beyond. This is where the magic happens.

You can't mandate discretionary performance. You can't require people to operate in that zone. They have to choose to go there.

So how do you get people to voluntarily operate in the Discretionary Performance Zone? You create the experiences that make them want to.

WHAT MAKES PEOPLE CHOOSE TO GIVE MORE

People choose to operate in the Discretionary Performance Zone when:

1. THEY KNOW WHAT MATTERS

Clarity about what success looks like. When people understand the result the team is trying to achieve and how their work contributes, they engage differently. Vague goals get minimal effort. Crystal clear goals that matter get discretionary effort.

2. THEY BELIEVE THEIR CONTRIBUTION MATTERS

If their experience has been that their contributions get ignored or dismissed, why would they contribute more? But if they have experienced that their ideas get implemented, their work gets recognized, and their effort makes a difference, they will give more.

3. THEY FEEL OWNERSHIP

When people feel like hired hands, they do what they're told. When they feel like owners, they do what needs to be done. The difference is whether they see themselves as responsible FOR the result or responsible TO deliver tasks.

4. THEY TRUST LEADERSHIP

If they don't trust you, they'll protect themselves by doing the minimum. If they trust you, they'll extend themselves because they believe you have their back.

5. THEY SEE OTHERS DOING IT

Discretionary performance is contagious. When people see their teammates going above and beyond — and being recognized for it — they're more likely to do the same.

THE TEAM THAT CHOSE TO GIVE MORE

I worked with a manufacturing team that was consistently hitting their production targets. Not exceeding them. Just hitting them. Exactly what was expected, nothing more.

The plant manager was frustrated. He knew the team was capable of more. But when he pushed for higher targets, he got resistance.

Here's what changed: Instead of setting top-down stretch goals, he brought the team together and showed them the business reality. The plant was at risk of losing a major contract because a competitor could deliver faster. If they lost the contract, layoffs were likely.

Then he asked: What would it take for us to match that delivery speed?

The team started problem-solving. Not because he told them to. Because they understood what was at stake and they had ownership of finding the solution.

Within two weeks, they had redesigned their process flow, eliminated three bottlenecks, and increased throughput by 23%. Not because the manager mandated it. Because they chose to.

What changed? Transparency about what mattered. Trust that their ideas would be implemented. Ownership of the solution. Recognition when they delivered. Those experiences created new beliefs. Those beliefs drove new actions. Those actions produced extraordinary results.

HOW TO DRAW OUT DISCRETIONARY PERFORMANCE

Five practices that create the experiences that make people want to operate in the Discretionary Performance Zone:

Paint a Crystal Clear Picture of What Matters. Don't just tell people what to do. Help them understand WHY it matters, WHAT success looks like, and HOW their work contributes.

When people can see the finish line and understand why crossing it matters, they move faster.

Ask, Don't Tell. Instead of 'Here is what you need to do,' try 'What do you think we should do?' or 'What is your recommendation?' When people co-create the solution, they own it.

Recognize Discretionary Effort Publicly. When someone goes above and beyond, acknowledge it publicly. Let everyone see that discretionary performance is noticed, valued, and celebrated.

Remove Obstacles. Nothing kills discretionary performance faster than bureaucracy and barriers. When people want to do more but systems prevent them, they stop trying. Your job is to clear the path.

Trust First. Give people latitude to make decisions. Let them try approaches their way. When you trust people, they rise to meet that trust. When you micromanage, they do the minimum to avoid being criticized.

DRAWING OUT TALENT WITHOUT POSITIONAL AUTHORITY

Everything we have discussed so far works whether you are a manager or not.

In fact, some of the best talent developers I have known had zero formal authority. They were individual contributors who made everyone around them better through influence, not authority.

You do not need a title to create experiences. You do not need formal authority to draw out talent in others. You just need to understand that every interaction you have with another person is an experience for them.

How to draw out talent through influence:

BE THE EXAMPLE

People watch what you do. When you operate in your Discretionary Performance Zone — when you go above and beyond, when you bring ideas and energy and ownership — others notice. Your actions create experiences for them that shape their beliefs about what is normal here.

ASK GREAT QUESTIONS

You do not need authority to ask, 'What if we tried this approach?' or 'How could we make this better?' or 'What would you do if there were no constraints?' Great questions create thinking. Thinking creates engagement. Engagement leads to discretionary performance.

OFFER HELP GENEROUSLY

When you help others succeed, you create powerful experiences. They experience: This person has my back. This person wants me to succeed. That belief drives the action of reciprocity — they want to help you succeed too.

RECOGNIZE OTHERS' CONTRIBUTIONS

You do not need a title to say, 'Great idea' or 'That approach really worked' or 'I learned something from how you handled that.' Recognition from peers is sometimes more powerful than recognition from bosses because it is freely given, not obligatory.

INVITE PEOPLE INTO SOLUTION-FINDING

Instead of complaining about problems, invite others to solve them with you. 'I am working on X challenge. Would you be willing to brainstorm with me?' This creates ownership and engagement without requiring authority.

BRAND YOU: EVERY ACTION IS DEVELOPING YOUR REPUTATION

Here is something most people miss: Every single action you take is creating your brand. Not the brand you think you have. The brand other people experience.

I call this Brand You. It is how others see you based on the experiences you create for them.

I use a demonstration in almost every keynote. I ask the audience to put their hands out in front of them, wide apart. I tell them on the count of three, we will all clap simultaneously. One... two...

I clap on two and a half. Not three.

And virtually everyone in the room follows my action — not my words.

Words are cheap. People will tolerate what you say. They will act on what they see you do. That is Brand You in action.

What you DO creates the experience. The experience creates the belief. The belief drives the action others take.

THE BRAND YOU PRINCIPLES

1. YOU ALWAYS HAVE A BRAND

Every person in your organization has a default brand — simply how other people see you. It is the result of all the experiences you have created for them. You cannot not have a brand. You can only choose whether to be intentional about it.

2. YOUR BRAND IS NOT WHAT YOU THINK IT IS

Your brand is what others experience. You may think you are collaborative. But if people experience you as dismissive in meetings, your brand is dismissive — not collaborative. What you intend does not matter. What they experience matters.

3. EVERY ACTION EITHER REINFORCES OR CHANGES YOUR BRAND

Every email you send, every meeting you attend, every conversation you have — it is creating an experience. That experience either confirms what people already believe about you or it is developing a new belief.

4. YOUR BRAND AFFECTS YOUR OPPORTUNITIES

When opportunities arise, managers give them to people with the brand they want. When teams form, people choose teammates with brands they trust. Your brand determines what doors open for you.

BUILDING THE BRAND YOU WANT

Know What Brand You Want. What do you want to be known for? Reliable? Innovative? Collaborative? Problem-solver? Pick 2-3 attributes that matter most to you.

Ask How You Are Actually Seen. This requires courage. Ask colleagues, your boss, your team: How would you describe working with me? The gap between how you want to be seen and how you are seen is your development opportunity.

Align Your Actions With Your Desired Brand. If you want to be known as collaborative but you dominate every meeting, your actions and your desired brand are misaligned. Close the gap.

Be Consistent. Your brand is built through repetition. One great meeting does not make you collaborative. Twenty great meetings start to build that brand.

Fix Brand Damage Quickly. You will make mistakes. Own them. Apologize. Create new positive experiences quickly. One bad experience can damage your brand. Ten good experiences can rebuild it.

MAYA DREW OUT TALENT. DAVID DID NOT.

Remember Maya and David from earlier in this chapter?

Maya built her brand through the experiences she created. She asked questions that made people think. She recognized contributions publicly. She helped people succeed. She trusted junior engineers with challenges. She removed obstacles.

All of those actions created experiences. Those experiences developed beliefs in others: My ideas matter. I can do this. I am valued. This team supports me.

Those beliefs drove actions: People contributed more. They took ownership. They operated in their Discretionary Performance Zone. Not because Maya had formal authority over all of them. Because the experiences she created made them want to.

David, for all his technical brilliance, created the opposite experiences. He dismissed ideas. He hoarded knowledge. He made people feel small. He worked in isolation.

Those experiences created beliefs: My ideas are not good enough. It is not safe to ask questions. Success here means not bothering David.

Those beliefs drove actions: People stayed quiet. They did the minimum. They avoided David when possible.

Same team. Same opportunities. Completely different outcomes. All because of the experiences each person created.

THE TALENT YOU ATTRACT MATTERS AS MUCH AS YOUR OWN TALENT

So far we've talked about building your own talent value. But here's something even more important:

The talent you surround yourself with matters as much as your own talent.

In the age of AI, individual brilliance matters less than collective capability. The problems worth solving, the opportunities worth pursuing, the innovations worth creating — they all require teams, not individuals.

THE A PLAYER MULTIPLIER EFFECT

There's a principle in organizational psychology: A players want to work with A players. B players hire C players.

Why? Because A players are secure enough in their own abilities that they're not threatened by other talented people. They know that working with great people makes them better.

B players feel threatened by A players, so they hire people less talented than themselves to protect their position. This creates a downward spiral of talent.

The talent you tolerate becomes the talent you attract.

If you tolerate low performers on your team, high performers
won't want to join you.

If you tolerate toxic behavior, great people will leave.

If you tolerate mediocrity, mediocrity is what you'll get.

But if you maintain high standards, attract and retain great people,
and create an environment where talent thrives — more talent wants to join you. Great talent attracts more great talent.
Which creates better results. Which attracts even more talent.

HOW TO ATTRACT A PLAYERS

Be an A Player Yourself. A players don't want to work with B
players. If you want to attract great talent, be great talent.
Work on your horizontal bar. Be Maya, not David.

Work on Interesting Problems. Great talent wants challenge,
impact, and learning. If you're working on boring, low-impact
problems, you won't attract the best people.

Create a Culture of Excellence. A players want to be pushed.
They want high standards. They want feedback. They want
to work in environments where excellence is expected and
mediocrity isn't tolerated.

Give Credit and Visibility. Great talent doesn't just want to do
great work. They want recognition for it. Share credit generously. Make heroes of your team members.

Remove Bad Apples Quickly. One toxic person, one chronic
underperformer, one person who brings everyone down —
they will drive away your A players faster than anything else.

YOUR NETWORK IS YOUR NET WORTH IN THE AGE OF AI

In the age of AI, this is more true than ever. But not for the reason most people think.

It's not about collecting business cards or LinkedIn connections. It's about building genuine relationships with talented people who know your work, trust your judgment, and want to collaborate with you.

THE FUTURE OF WORK IS PROJECT-BASED, NOT JOB-BASED

The traditional career path — work for one company for years, climb the ladder, retire with a pension — is already dying. AI is accelerating its death.

The new career path looks like this: Assemble talented teams for specific projects, deliver exceptional results, disband, reassemble in different configurations for the next project.

Think Hollywood. Directors, actors, cinematographers — they don't work for one studio. They work on projects. The best people work together repeatedly because they know each other, trust each other, and produce great results together.

This is becoming the norm across industries. Contract work, project-based teams, fractional executives, temporary collaborations around specific challenges.

In this world, your ability to assemble talented people quickly becomes your most valuable asset.

This shift is not theoretical. In the same week I completed this manuscript, more than 600,000 jobs were cut — the vast majority of them permanent, full-time roles eliminated by AI automation.

Many of those people had deep technical skills and decades of experience. What most of them lacked were the networks that would allow them to reassemble in a new configuration and deliver value in a new context. The professionals who will navigate this landscape most successfully are not the ones waiting for the next full-time job to find them. They are the ones whose networks are so strong that opportunities find them first.

BUILDING A TALENT NETWORK THAT MATTERS

Focus on Depth, Not Breadth. Better to have 20 people who would take your call and collaborate with you than 2,000 LinkedIn connections who barely remember you. Quality beats quantity massively.

Give Before You Ask. The strongest networks are built on reciprocity. Help people without keeping score. Make introductions. Share opportunities. Offer your expertise. When you eventually need help, people remember.

Stay in Touch Without Agenda. Don't only reach out when you need something. Check in periodically. Share interesting articles. Congratulate people on wins. Show genuine interest in their work. This builds relationships, not transactions.

Be Known for Something. You want to be the person others think of when they need X. Be excellent at something specific so people know when to call you.

Work With Great People When You Can. Every project is an audition for the next one. When you work with talented people and do great work together, those relationships compound. They become your go-to collaborators.

Maya built a network over 10 years. When she left that company to start a consulting practice, she had 30 people she could call who would work with her on projects. Within 6 months, she had more work than she could handle because her network trusted her and wanted to work with her.

David had no network. Despite his technical brilliance, when he left — was fired — he struggled to find work because nobody wanted to vouch for him. His talent was his only asset, and talent alone isn't enough.

TALENT: YOUR THIRD LAYER OF KRYPTONITE

In the age of AI, technical skills are table stakes. They get you in the game. But they don't keep you in the game.

What keeps you in the game is your talent value — the combination of technical excellence and human skills that make you someone worth working with, someone who multiplies others' effectiveness, someone who attracts great talent.

David had technical skills but no talent value. Maya had both. That's why Maya thrived and David didn't.

Remember the five practices:

Become a multiplier, not just a contributor
Master the art of translation
Build trust through reliability
Develop judgment, not just skills
Be someone people want to work with

And remember: The talent you attract matters as much as your own talent. Build a network of great people who trust you and want to work with you.

The future doesn't belong to brilliant individuals.
It belongs to talented people who can assemble talented teams
to solve problems that matter.

CHAPTER 5

Those prepared need not fear the forces at work.

You've now got three ingredients of your Kryptonite defense: IDEAS, SPEED, and TALENT.

But ideas, speed, and talent mean nothing if you blend into the crowd — if you're indistinguishable from everyone else doing similar work.

That's why the fourth ingredient is DISTINCTION.

And that's where we're going next.

. . .

COMING UP IN CHAPTER 6:

In Chapter 6, we'll tackle the fourth ingredient of your Kryptonite defense: DISTINCTION.

You'll discover why being good isn't good enough, how to stand out in a sea of sameness, and why your personal brand matters more than ever when AI can replicate technical competence.

Because here's the truth: In a world where everyone has access to the same AI tools, the same information, and the same capabilities, distinction is the only sustainable advantage. Either you're distinct, or you're extinct.

DISTINCTION

*The Fourth Ingredient
of Your Kryptonite Defense*

I needed to change auto insurance companies last month. Nothing dramatic, just my old provider raised rates and I figured I should shop around.

So I did what anyone does now. I went online and started comparing providers.

Six major companies. All household names. All with excellent ratings. I pulled quotes from every one of them.

And here is what I discovered: They were all offering essentially the same product, priced almost identically, with the same coverage levels, the same claims process, very similar customer service ratings.

It was like choosing between six versions of the exact same thing. The differences were so minor they were almost meaningless. Slight variations in deductibles. Tiny differences in annual cost. But fundamentally, identical.

Nothing made any of them stand out. Nothing caused me to think, I have to choose this one.

Then it hit me. This is not just insurance.

I have been standing on stages since 1998 warning Fortune 50 executives about what I call the Surplus Society. Back then, they nodded politely and wondered if I was being dramatic. Today they call me back.

THE SEA OF SAMENESS

The same thing is true with:

Internet providers. Same speeds, same prices, same reliability claims.

Banking services. Same accounts, same rates, same mobile apps.

Phone services. Same plans, same coverage maps, same upgrade offers.

Medical providers. Same credentials, same insurance accepted, same wait times.

Contractors. Same licenses, same warranties, same promises.

Auto repair shops. Same certifications, same parts, same turnaround times.

Mortgage companies. Same rates, same terms, same approval process.

Accounting firms. Same services, same software, same tax strategies.

And here is the uncomfortable truth: The same is true for employees.

When a hiring manager looks at resumes, they see similar educational backgrounds, similar work experience, similar skill sets, similar career trajectories. Everyone looks the same on paper.

We live in what I call the Surplus Society. A surplus of similar companies, employing similar people, with similar educational backgrounds, coming up with similar ideas, producing similar things, with similar prices and similar quality, providing similar service.

This is not hyperbole. This is reality.

I sat in a room with twelve senior executives who had just completed a comprehensive benchmarking exercise. Every dimension. Quality. Service. Price. Responsiveness. Speed. They compared themselves to their six primary competitors on every measure that mattered.

The results were stunning in the worst possible way. They scored within three points of every competitor on every single dimension. They were indistinguishable. The silence in that room was deafening. One executive finally said what everyone was thinking: If we are this hard to tell apart, why would anyone choose us?

That question is the most important one any professional or organization can ask. And most never do.

SO HOW DID I CHOOSE MY INSURANCE COMPANY?

With everything being essentially the same, I had to make a decision somehow. And I realized what actually influenced my choice:

The experience one company created for me.

One provider had an agent who returned my call within an hour. Another took three days. One had a website that made getting a quote simple. Another required me to fill out the same information on four different screens. One sent me a personalized video explaining my coverage options. The others sent generic emails.

The product was the same. The price was nearly identical. The coverage was equivalent.

But the experience was dramatically different.

And that experience — that is what made one company distinct. That is what earned my business.

This is the uncomfortable reality we all face: When products, services, and qualifications become commoditized, when everyone can do basically the same thing at basically the same level, distinction comes down to the experience you create.

WHY THIS MATTERS MORE THAN EVER

Remember the 7-Sided Pincer Movement we discussed in Chapter 1? ERP and SAP. White collar robots. Globalization. Outsourcing. The internet. Disruptive competition. And AI.

Every one of those forces is accelerating the commoditization problem. Making it easier for everyone to be good. And harder for anyone to be distinct.

Consider this scenario:

You need to hire a software engineer. You post the job. You get 200 applications. Half of them have computer science degrees from good schools. Most have 3-5 years of experience. They have all worked with the same technologies. They have all completed similar projects.

How do you choose?

Or flip it around. You are one of those 200 applicants. You have a good degree. Solid experience. Relevant skills. So does everyone else.

How do you get chosen?

The answer is not by being good. Good is the baseline. Good is table stakes. Good gets you into the pool of 200.

The answer is by being distinct.

THE BLINDSPOT WE KEEP REPEATING

Philadelphia. October 1956.

The longshoremen on the docks saw containerization coming. New technology. New methods. The writing was on the wall. And most of them assumed they would adapt. They had decades of experience. They knew the work. They believed their value was in what they did.

It was not. Their value was in who they were — their judgment, their relationships, their ability to think through problems no machine could anticipate. But they never made that case. They kept selling the same thing they had always sold: the ability to move cargo.

The dock did not need strong backs anymore. It needed people who could think, adapt, and lead machines.

Same disruption. Same blindspot. Seventy years later, white-collar professionals are standing on the same dock, making the same assumption. My value is in what I do. Not who I am.

That assumption is the most dangerous one you can make right now.

THE AI THREAT TO DISTINCTION

And here is where it gets even more challenging.

AI is about to make comparison shopping instantaneous and comprehensive. Right now, I can ask my AI assistant:

Find me auto insurance. Compare every provider. Show me the coverage differences. Calculate the total cost over five years including all fees. Show me customer satisfaction ratings. Give me the three best options for my specific situation.

The AI does this in seconds. Perfect comparison. Complete information. Optimized recommendation.

Now think about what this means:

What happens to Amazon, or any product or service provider, when my AI can find any product or service I need, compare it to every option available, and purchase it with one click?

When AI eliminates information asymmetry, when every customer has perfect information about every option, the only thing left to compete on is:

Price. Which starts a race to the bottom that nobody wins.

Or distinction. Something that makes you memorably different.

I have watched six other forces do this same thing before AI arrived as the accelerant. The ERP wave of the 1990s. Globalization in the 2000s. Digital disruption in the 2010s. The pattern is identical every time. First: denial. Then: rationalization. Then: urgency. The professionals who win are never the ones who waited for the urgency phase. They are the ones who built their distinction before the disruption arrived at their door.

I was not being dramatic when I warned about this for 27 years. I was early. There is a difference. And there has always been a defense — which is what the rest of this chapter is about.

There is also a layer to this that most people have not yet considered. AI will not only help customers compare what exists — it will shape what they perceive as worth considering in the first place. Elon Musk raised a question that deserves serious thought: If you have a super intelligent AI that is capable of writing incredibly well, figuring out what is more convincing to people, and then it enters social media — how would we even know? The implication is direct. In a world where AI shapes perception and preference at scale, distinction built on authentic human experience — who you genuinely are, the real value you deliver, the honest proof you can provide — becomes not just an advantage but a shield.

Distinction is not optional anymore. It is survival.

QUALITY AND SERVICE ARE NOT ENOUGH

For decades, we were told: Deliver quality. Provide great service. That is how you win.

That was true. Once.

But quality and service are now the price of entry. If you do not deliver quality, you are not even in the game. But quality alone will not make you distinct.

Think about cars. Thirty years ago, you could tell brands apart from a block away. A Cadillac looked nothing like a Honda looked nothing like a BMW.

Now? Drive down any street. What do you see? SUVs that all look remarkably similar. Sedans that are nearly indistinguishable. Even luxury brands and economy brands are converging in appearance.

Everything is better. Safety features that used to be luxury options are now standard. Reliability that was once exceptional is now expected. The quality gap has closed.

While everything may be better, it is also increasingly the same.

This is true across industries. Hotels all offer similar amenities. Airlines all provide similar service levels. Retailers all have similar return policies. Consultants all use similar methodologies.

The quality bar has risen for everyone. Which means quality no longer differentiates anyone.

FROM SERVICE TO EXPERIENCES

So if quality and service are not enough, what creates distinction?

Experiences.

Experiences are as distinct from services as services are from goods.

A good is a tangible product. A service is an intangible action. An experience is a memorable event.

Goods are standardized. Services can be improved. Experiences are inherently personal and memorable.

Let me show you what I mean.

The Starbucks Experience

People pay five dollars or more for coffee at Starbucks. You can get basically the same coffee at a gas station for two dollars. Same caffeine. Similar taste. Faster service.

So why Starbucks?

Here is how Starbucks describes it: We have identified a third place. And I really believe that sets us apart. The third place is that place that is not work or home. It is the place our customers come for refuge.

Starbucks does not sell coffee. They sell an experience. A place to work without being at work. A place to meet without the formality of an office or the casualness of home. A place that feels comfortable, sounds pleasant, smells appealing.

The coffee is the product. The third place is the experience. People pay for the experience.

The Harley-Davidson Experience

Harley-Davidson does not describe their business as selling motorcycles. Here is how they describe what they sell:

What we sell is the ability for a 43-year-old accountant to dress in black leather, ride through small towns, and have people be afraid of him.

That is not a product description. That is an experience description.

Harley understands that people are not buying transportation. They are buying transformation. The experience of being someone different. The feeling of freedom and rebellion and power.

Honda makes excellent motorcycles. So does Yamaha. Often better performing, more reliable, less expensive than Harley.

But Honda does not have the same cult following. Because Honda sells motorcycles. Harley sells an experience.

The Progressive Experience

Progressive Insurance figured this out. In a commoditized market where every insurance company offers basically the same coverage at basically the same price, how do you stand out?

Progressive decided: We do not sell insurance. We sell speed.

Fast quotes. Fast claims. Fast service. The experience of speed became their distinction.

It is not about the product. Everyone has the product. It is about the experience of interacting with the company.

WHAT EXPERIENCE ARE YOU CREATING?

These are companies with marketing budgets and brand teams. But the principle applies to you as an individual professional too.

Every interaction you have with another person creates an experience. That experience shapes how they see you. And how they see you determines whether they want to work with you, hire you, promote you, or recommend you.

Remember from Chapter 5: Every action you take is an experience for everyone watching you. It is either reinforcing what they already believe about you, or you are fostering a new belief they will hold about you.

This is Brand You in action.

Your brand is not what you say about yourself. Your brand is the sum of the experiences you create for others.

And in the age of AI, when technical skills become less differentiated, when information becomes universally accessible, when automation handles the routine work, your brand — the experience you create — becomes your primary source of distinction.

BRAND YOU: A DEPRECIATING ASSET THAT REQUIRES INVESTMENT

Here is the uncomfortable truth that most people miss:

You are a depreciating asset.

Your knowledge becomes outdated. Your skills become less relevant. Your network becomes less active. Your reputation fades if you are not actively reinforcing it.

This is not pessimism. This is reality in a world that changes faster every year.

Think about a car. The day you drive it off the lot, it starts depreciating. Every mile you drive, every day that passes, its value decreases unless you actively maintain and invest in it.

You are no different. Your value in the marketplace is constantly depreciating unless you are actively investing in renewal.

The Investment Requirements

Just like any asset, you need a formal renewal investment plan. Not a vague intention to get better. A formal plan with specific investments:

YOU MUST INVEST

Time. Money. Energy. Focus.

You must invest in learning new skills. Not just in your core area, but in adjacent areas that make you more valuable. If you are a data analyst, invest in storytelling. If you are an engineer, invest in business strategy. If you are in sales, invest in understanding AI.

You must invest in expanding your network. Relationships depreciate if you do not maintain them. People change jobs, move cities, forget about you if you are not actively staying connected.

You must invest in your visibility. The best people get overlooked all the time because nobody knows what they are capable of. You need to invest in making your work, your capabilities, and your value visible to decision makers.

THAT PLAN MUST BE FORMAL

Not something you get to when you have time. A formal, scheduled commitment.

What are you learning this quarter? What skill are you developing? What course are you taking? What certification are you pursuing?

Who are you connecting with this month? What events are you attending? What conversations are you initiating?

What are you creating to demonstrate your expertise? What are you writing? What are you presenting? What are you building?

Vague intentions do not stop depreciation. Specific investments do.

YOU MUST SCHEDULE ROUTINE BRAND YOU AUDITS

Every six months, ask yourself:

What experiences am I creating? Are they building the brand I want or eroding it?

What is my dramatic difference right now? Has it evolved or become stale?

What overt benefit am I providing? Is it still relevant or has the market moved?

Can I prove my value with recent examples? Or am I relying on accomplishments from three years ago?

Who knows what I am capable of? Am I visible to the right people?

These audits are not optional. Your brand is always changing, either intentionally because you are managing it or unintentionally because you are neglecting it.

Choose intention.

THE FOUR QUESTIONS THAT DEFINE DISTINCTION

My insurance shopping experience — and 27 years of watching professionals navigate disruption — forced me to define four critical questions. Questions that every professional needs to answer if they want to be distinct rather than extinct:

1. What is your dramatic difference?

Not your minor variation. Not your slight improvement. Your dramatic difference.

This is not about being incrementally better. It is about being fundamentally different in a way that matters.

When someone asks, Why should I work with you instead of the 50 other qualified people, what is your answer?

Because I am good at my job? So is everyone else.

Because I work hard? Expected.

Because I have the right credentials? Table stakes.

Your dramatic difference is the thing about you that makes people think, That is not something I get anywhere else.

Maybe it is your approach. Maybe it is your perspective. Maybe it is how you make people feel. Maybe it is the unique combination of skills you bring that nobody else has.

But it has to be dramatic. Not subtle. Not slight. Dramatic.

2. What is your overt benefit?

Your dramatic difference means nothing if people cannot see how it benefits them.

Overt means obvious. Clear. Unmistakable.

It is not enough to be different. You have to be different in a way that solves a problem someone actually has or creates value someone actually wants.

Remember Progressive? Their dramatic difference is speed. Their overt benefit is: You get your claim resolved fast so you can get back to your life.

Harley? Dramatic difference is the culture and identity. Overt benefit is: You feel like a different person when you ride.

What problem do you solve? What value do you create? And can someone understand that benefit within 10 seconds of meeting you?

If your answer is vague or complicated or requires explanation, you do not have an overt benefit yet. You have a subtle benefit. Which means it is not benefiting you.

3. How can you prove it?

Anyone can claim to be different. Anyone can talk about benefits. But can you prove it?

Proof comes in many forms:

Results you have delivered. Projects you have completed. Problems you have solved. People who will vouch for you. Work that speaks for itself.

When I was evaluating insurance companies, one agent sent me a video testimonial from three of her clients explaining how she had helped them through difficult claims. That was proof.

Another sent me generic marketing materials about how great their company was. That was not proof. That was noise.

What evidence can you provide that you actually deliver on your dramatic difference and overt benefit?

If you cannot answer that question with specific, concrete examples, then you do not have distinction yet. You have aspiration.

4. Who experiences it?

Your dramatic difference means nothing if the wrong people are witnessing it.

Distinction requires an audience. Specifically, the audience that makes decisions about your career. Are you delivering your best work where the right people can see it? Or are you creating extraordinary experiences in rooms where nobody with influence is watching?

I have met professionals with genuine mastery, clear overt benefits, and compelling proof — who are completely invisible to the people who could advance their careers. They are excellent in private. Distinction requires excellence in public.

Ask yourself: Does my boss know my three biggest wins from last quarter? Do the decision-makers in my organization know what I am uniquely capable of? Does my network know what problems I solve?

If the answer to any of those is no, you have a visibility problem, not a distinction problem. And visibility is something you can fix today.

THE ONLY ONE WHO DOES WHAT YOU DO

Jerry Garcia, the legendary guitarist and leader of The Grateful Dead, understood distinction better than most business people ever will. Here is what he said:

You do not merely want to be the best of the best. You want to be considered the only ones who do what you do.

Read that again. Not the best. The only.

Best is a competition. Only is a category of one.

The Grateful Dead did not try to be the best rock band. They created a completely unique experience. The improvisational performances. The loyal fan community. The tape-trading culture. The way they approached touring and connecting with audiences.

They were not the best rock band. They were the only Grateful Dead.

That is distinction.

You do not need to be the best software engineer, the best project manager, the best sales professional. You need to be the only one who brings your unique combination of skills, perspective, and approach to solving the problems you solve.

BRAND YOU: THE FIVE KEY ELEMENTS

Building a distinct personal brand requires attention to five key elements. These are not personality traits you either have or do not have. These are choices you make about how you show up in the world.

1. DISTINCTION

This is what we have been discussing. What makes you memorably different? Not better. Different in a way that matters.

Your distinction comes from the unique combination of what you know, how you think, what you have experienced, and how you apply all of that to solve problems.

Nobody else has your exact combination. The question is: Are you making that combination visible and valuable to others?

2. EXCELLENCE

Distinction without excellence is just novelty. And novelty wears off fast.

Excellence means you deliver consistently high-quality work. Every time. Not just when it is convenient or when people are watching.

Excellence creates wow experiences in everything you do. It means you never tarnish your brand with sloppy work, missed deadlines, or half-hearted efforts.

Remember: One bad experience can damage your brand. Excellence is not a sometimes thing. It is an always thing.

3. EMOTIONAL SIGNATURE

This is how people feel when they interact with you. And feelings are what people remember.

Maya Angelou said it perfectly: People will forget what you said, forget what you did, but people will never forget how you made them feel.

Do people feel energized after working with you? Confident? Frustrated? Anxious? Inspired?

Your emotional signature is the consistent feeling you create. And that feeling becomes part of your brand whether you intend it or not.

Choose intentionally what emotional signature you want to create. Then create experiences that consistently deliver that feeling.

4. TRUSTWORTHINESS

Without trust, nothing else matters. You can be distinct, excellent, and create great emotional experiences. But if people cannot trust you, they will not work with you.

Trust comes from consistency between what you say and what you do. From following through on commitments. From being honest even when it costs you.

Trust is built slowly through many small actions. It is destroyed quickly through one significant breach.

Your brand depends on trustworthiness more than any other element. Protect it fiercely.

5. CONSISTENCY

Brands are built through repetition. People need to see your distinction, experience your excellence, feel your emotional signature, and witness your trustworthiness multiple times before they truly believe it.

One great interaction does not make a brand. Twenty great interactions start to build one.

This is where many people fail. They are excellent sometimes. Distinct occasionally. Trustworthy when it is convenient.

But brands require consistency. Who you are on Tuesday when you are tired must match who you are on Monday when you are fresh. The experience you create for an intern must match the experience you create for an executive.

Consistency is how distinction becomes your reputation.

YOUR FUTURE WORK BRAND YOU SURVIVAL KIT

Theory without tools is just inspiration. Here is your toolkit.

In the age of AI, with the 7-Sided Pincer Movement threatening 70-90% of jobs, certain attributes have become non-negotiable for professional survival and distinction.

These are not nice-to-haves. These are must-haves. Your survival kit for staying distinct and valuable when AI can do much of what you currently do.

MASTERY

Be the best or absurdly good at something. Have an area of focus where you are known as the go-to person.

This does not mean being the world expert. It means being the person your team, your company, your network thinks of when they need that specific expertise.

Mastery creates distinction because most people are generalists trying to be decent at everything. When you are exceptional at something specific, you become irreplaceable for that thing.

What is your mastery area? If you do not have one, develop one. Intentionally.

MANAGE TO LEGACY

All of your work should be memorable, braggable, and have the wow factor.

When you finish a project, can people tell that story to others? Is it worth bragging about? Does it create a wow response?

If not, you are creating forgettable work. And forgettable work does not build distinction. It builds nothing.

Manage every project, every interaction, every deliverable with this question: Will this be part of the legacy I want to leave? Will people remember this?

If the answer is no, elevate it until the answer is yes.

UNIQUE SELLING PROPOSITION

This is your dramatic difference expressed in 10 words or less.

Your remarkable point of view that someone can understand and remember in a single sentence.

Most people cannot articulate their unique selling proposition. When asked what makes you different, they ramble. They list credentials. They describe their job responsibilities.

That is not a USP. That is noise.

Your USP should be crisp, clear, and compelling. Ten words or less. If you cannot articulate it that concisely, you do not have clarity on your distinction yet.

NETWORKING OBSESSION

Networking is not optional. It is essential in every aspect of your life and career.

Your network determines your opportunities. Your network amplifies your visibility. Your network validates your expertise. Your network catches you when you need help.

And in the age of AI, when technical work becomes more automated, your network becomes even more valuable. Because relationships are the one thing AI cannot automate.

Be obsessed with building, maintaining, and leveraging your network. Not in a transactional way. In a genuine, value-creating way.

The strongest networks are built on giving first, connecting people, and creating value for others without expecting immediate return.

ENTREPRENEURIAL INSTINCT

Have an obsessive eye for opportunity to strengthen your brand.

Entrepreneurs see possibilities where others see problems. They see opportunities where others see obstacles. They see ways to create value where others see constraints.

You need that instinct. Not to start a company necessarily. But to approach your career entrepreneurially.

Ask: Where is the opportunity here? How can I create more value? What problem can I solve that nobody else is solving? How can I position myself for the next wave of change?

People with entrepreneurial instinct do not wait for permission or perfect conditions. They see what needs to happen and make it happen.

CEO/LEADER/BUSINESSPERSON MINDSET

Think like a CEO. You are CEO, Me, Inc. Available 24/7 to lead your life, your career, and your destiny.

This means taking full ownership and accountability for your professional trajectory. Not waiting for your boss to develop you. Not hoping your company will take care of you. Not assuming loyalty will be rewarded.

You are running a business. The business of you. And like any CEO, you need strategy, you need to manage resources, you need to make tough decisions, and you need to drive results.

Nobody cares more about your career than you do. Nobody should. Treat it that way.

MASTER OF IMPROV

Be willing to own it all. From Chief Strategist to Chief Toilet Scrubber.

Distinction does not come from only doing the prestigious work or the work you think is beneath you. It comes from being willing to do whatever needs to be done to deliver results.

The best professionals have range. They can think strategically and execute tactically. They can lead and they can follow. They can do the glamorous work and the grunt work.

This is what mastery of improv means. You adapt to what the situation requires. You do not hide behind your title or your job description. You solve problems.

SENSE OF HUMOR

Business people are way too serious. A sense of humor signals confidence, relatability, and resilience.

It means you are willing to screw up, shrug it off, learn, and move on. You do not take yourself so seriously that you cannot admit mistakes or laugh at the absurdity we all face sometimes.

People want to work with people who are human. Humor makes you human. It makes you memorable. It makes difficult situations more manageable.

This is not about being a comedian. It is about not being rigid, defensive, or brittle. AI can process information. Only humans can bring levity to tense situations.

COMFORTABLE IN YOUR SKIN

Bring your interesting self to work. Not a corporate automaton version of yourself. Your actual self.

Your quirks, your interests, your perspectives — they make you distinct. When you hide them to fit in, you make yourself more generic. More replaceable.

The professionals who stand out are comfortable being themselves. They do not perform a role. They show up as actual people with personalities and passions.

This is what makes people remember you. This is what makes them say, We need to work with that person, not We need to work with someone like that person.

INTENSE UNRELENTING APPETITE
FOR TECHNOLOGY

This is not an option. It is survival.

You must be obsessed with understanding AI and emerging technologies. Not at an expert level. At a user level. At a how-can-this-make-me-more-valuable level.

The people who stay employed are not the ones fighting technology or ignoring it. They are the ones leveraging it to multiply their capabilities.

Treat technology fluency like breathing. Necessary. Continuous. Non-negotiable.

EMBRACE MARKETING: YOU ARE YOUR OWN CHIEF STORYTELLING OFFICER

Many professionals think marketing is beneath them. That good work should speak for itself.

That is a career-limiting belief.

Good work that nobody knows about is invisible work. And invisible work does not create distinction.

You are your own CSO, Chief Storytelling Officer. Nobody is going to tell your story for you. Nobody is going to promote your capabilities for you. Nobody is going to make you visible for you.

You need to get comfortable sharing your wins, explaining your approach, demonstrating your expertise. Not obnoxiously. But consistently.

The best people do not always win. The best people who are also visible win.

OBSESSED WITH RENEWAL: YOU ARE THE CLO, CHIEF LEARNING OFFICER OF YOU

Learn something new every single day or you will become obsolete.

That is not hyperbole. The half-life of skills is shrinking. What made you valuable two years ago may be table stakes today. What makes you valuable today may be automated tomorrow.

You are your own CLO, Chief Learning Officer. It is your responsibility to stay current, develop new capabilities, and evolve your expertise.

If you are not actively learning, you are passively becoming less valuable. There is no standing still. You are either growing or shrinking.

OUTWORK AND OVER-DELIVER

Mediocrity is unacceptable. Distinction requires you to be exceptional.

This means outworking your competition and over-delivering on every commitment. It means doing more than required, going beyond expectations, and refusing to settle for good enough.

Jerry Garcia said it: You want to be considered the only ones who do what you do. That does not happen by doing the minimum.

Excellence is not a sometimes thing. It is an always thing. And excellence combined with exceptional effort creates unstoppable distinction.

EXCELLENCE ALWAYS

Create wow experiences in everything you do. Never tarnish your brand with mediocre work.

Every interaction is an audition for the next opportunity. Every project is a demonstration of your capabilities. Every email, every meeting, every deliverable either strengthens your brand or weakens it.

There are no throwaway moments. There is no this-does-not-really-matter work. Everything matters. Everything contributes to the experience you create. Everything shapes your distinction.

PUTTING IT ALL TOGETHER

These 14 attributes are not a wish list. They are a survival kit.

In a world where AI can do much of what you currently do, where 70-90% of jobs are at risk from the 7-Sided Pincer Movement, these attributes are what keep you valuable, relevant, and distinct.

But here is what most people miss:

Having these attributes is not enough. You have to make them visible. You have to create experiences that demonstrate them. You have to build a brand around them.

This brings us back to where we started. With my insurance shopping experience and the realization that experiences are what create distinction.

WHAT EXPERIENCE ARE YOU CREATING RIGHT NOW?

Every interaction you have today is creating an experience for someone. That experience is shaping their belief about you. That belief is building or eroding your distinction.

Right now, what experience are you creating for:

Your boss? Do they experience you as someone who solves problems or creates them? Someone who takes ownership or deflects responsibility? Someone who makes their job easier or harder?

Your colleagues? Do they experience you as someone who elevates the team or drags it down? Someone who shares credit or hoards it? Someone who makes work more enjoyable or more stressful?

Your clients or customers? Do they experience you as someone who truly understands their needs or just pushes products? Someone who delivers more than promised or makes excuses? Someone they want to work with again or someone they hope to avoid?

Your network? Do they experience you as someone who creates value for others or only takes? Someone who connects people or isolates? Someone worth staying connected to or someone to forget about?

These experiences accumulate. Day by day. Interaction by interaction. They build your brand. They define your distinction. They determine whether you are seen as indispensable or replaceable.

DISTINCT OR EXTINCT: YOUR CHOICE

When I was shopping for insurance, I had to choose one company out of six essentially identical options. The one I chose was not better. It was distinct. It created a better experience.

Every day, people are making similar choices about you. Hiring managers choosing between candidates. Managers choosing who to promote. Clients choosing who to work with. Colleagues choosing who to collaborate with.

You are always competing against people with similar credentials, similar experience, similar capabilities. The question is never can you do the job. The question is why should they choose you.

The answer is distinction. Not perfection. Not credentials. Not seniority. Distinction.

And distinction comes from the experiences you create, the value you deliver, the brand you build, and the intentional choices you make every single day about who you are and how you show up.

In the insurance commodity market, one company stood out because of the experience they created. In the professional commodity market, you stand out the same way.

Build your dramatic difference. Deliver your overt benefit. Prove it with results. Make sure the right people witness it. Create experiences that people remember. Invest in your renewal. Develop your survival kit attributes. Be consistent. Be excellent. Be trust-worthy.

Those prepared need not fear the forces at work.

Be distinct. Because the alternative is extinction.

The choice has always been yours. It is just more urgent now.

• • •

COMING UP IN CHAPTER 7: LEADERSHIP AT ALL LEVELS

You have built your ideas muscle. You have developed speed. You have multiplied talent in yourself and others. You have created distinction.

Now comes the ingredient that ties everything together: Leadership.

Not leadership as a title. Leadership as a choice. Leadership as the ability to cultivate a culture where people voluntarily give their best work, where accountability is the norm, where change is embraced rather than feared.

In Chapter 7, we will explore the fifth ingredient of your Kryptonite defense. Because in the age of AI, leadership at all levels is what separates thriving organizations from extinct ones.

LEADERSHIP AT ALL LEVELS

*The Fifth Ingredient
of Your Kryptonite Defense*

SARAH DID NOT WAIT FOR PERMISSION

Sarah was not a manager. She had no direct reports. She was a mid-level analyst at a manufacturing company that was struggling with quality issues.

Production delays were mounting. Customer complaints were increasing. The engineering team blamed operations. Operations blamed engineering. Everyone pointed fingers. Nobody took ownership.

Sarah could have kept her head down. Focused on her spreadsheets. Let the managers figure it out. That is what most people do when they see organizational dysfunction and lack the authority to fix it.

But Sarah did something different.

She started asking questions. Not accusatory questions. Curious questions. She asked engineers: What would you need from operations to solve this faster? She asked operations: What information from engineering would help you prevent these issues?

Then she did something even more unusual. She organized an informal lunch meeting. No agenda. No PowerPoint. Just pizza and a simple question: What if we could fix this together?

Twelve people showed up. Engineers and operations folks who had barely spoken to each other in months sat around a conference room table.

Sarah did not present a solution. She facilitated a conversation. She asked what they saw. What they needed. What small experiment they could try.

By the end of lunch, the team had identified three bottlenecks and committed to testing two process changes. No executive mandate. No formal project plan. Just people choosing to solve a problem together.

Six weeks later, quality issues had dropped 40%. Production delays were down 30%. The plant manager asked Sarah what she had done.

"I did not do anything. I just helped people see that we could solve this if we worked together."

• • •

THE RESULTS MODEL AND LEADERSHIP

Before we go further, I want to name a framework that runs underneath every leadership principle in this chapter. You encountered it briefly in Chapter 2. Here it needs its own moment, because it is the foundation everything else in this chapter is built on.

It is called the Results Model.

EXPERIENCES → BELIEFS → ACTIONS → RESULTS

Every result in your professional life, every outcome, every relationship, every career trajectory, flows from this sequence. Your

Experiences shape your Beliefs. Your Beliefs drive your Actions. Your Actions produce your Results.

I have used a simple exercise to introduce this model for over 27 years, in rooms from NASA to Fortune 50 boardrooms, and the response is always the same. I ask everyone to pair up and compete in a hand-push game. The object is to score points. When I say go, the room explodes into activity. Some pairs score dozens of points. Some score zero. All 400 people in the room received the exact same instructions, from the same person, at the same time. And every single pair played it differently.

Why?

Because they interpreted the instructions differently. Some believed winning meant cooperation, partner with your counterpart and rack up points together. Others believed winning meant domination, beat the person in front of you. Same experience. Different belief. Completely different action. Completely different result.

That is the Results Model in six seconds.

It is the belief you took into the situation that drove your action, that produced your result. Not your intelligence. Not your experience level. Not your effort. Your belief.

I have shared this model with people around the globe for 27 years, at every level of every type of organization. And I consistently get people calling me back months later saying, Mike, that simple model changed my life. Not because it is complicated. Because it is true. And because once you see it, you cannot unsee it.

Where Organizations Focus — and Why They Stay Stuck

Here is the most important practical application of the Results Model for leaders.

When a team, department, or organization is not achieving the results they want, where do they almost always focus their energy? At the Action layer. Action plans. Policies. Procedures. Telling people what to do, when to do it, and how to do it. Enforcing compliance.

And here is the problem with that. When you are standing over someone enforcing compliance, they comply. When you walk across the street to a different building, they revert. Because they have not changed their Belief. They are still acting off the same mental model they always had. You changed the action temporarily. You did not change the thinking that produces the action.

If you find yourself spending most of your leadership energy at the Action layer, telling, reminding, enforcing, chasing, that is a signal. A big, red, neon, blinking signal that says, there are Beliefs in this culture that are holding you back. You are stuck at the action layer. Telling people what to do. Enforcing compliance. You are not dealing with a performance problem. You are dealing with a belief problem.

The way your team thinks and acts is your culture. Financial results, operational results, customer results, employee results — all of it flows from the way people think and act. If you want better results, you do not need better action plans. You need to change what people believe.

Most performance improvement efforts focus on Actions and Results. The Results Model says, go deeper. If you want different Results, you need different Actions. If you want different Actions, you need to change the Beliefs driving them. And if you want to change the Beliefs, you need to understand what Experiences created them, and then intentionally create new ones.

This is why leadership is harder than management. Management operates at the Action layer. Leadership operates at the Belief layer. And you cannot reach the Belief layer from a spreadsheet or a performance review. You reach it through the experiences you create for the people around you.

Remember, everything you do is an experience for everybody watching you. Every single action you take is either reinforcing what they already believe about you or your team, or creating a new belief they will hold. Are those beliefs helping you get the results you want? Are they impeding progress?

Leadership Is a Choice, Not a Position

Sarah, the analyst from the opening of this chapter who took ownership of a cross-functional quality problem without any formal authority, was not operating from a job description. She was operating from a belief, that problems visible to her were problems that belonged to her, at least in part. That waiting for someone with a title to solve them was not a strategy. That leadership was something she could choose, right now, from exactly where she was.

That belief is the foundation of LEADERSHIP AT ALL LEVELS. And it is available to every professional in your organization, if the culture makes it safe to act on.

The rest of this chapter is about how to build that belief in yourself, and how to create the conditions where others can build it too.

. . .

THE LEADERSHIP MYTH

Most people think leadership looks like this: A title. A corner office. People who report to you. The authority to make decisions and expect compliance.

That is not leadership. That is management. And management without leadership is just people with titles telling other people what to do.

Real leadership looks like Sarah. Someone who sees a problem and chooses to act. Someone who influences without authority. Someone who creates the experiences that make people want to contribute, collaborate, and take ownership.

Leadership is not a position. Leadership is a choice.

You can lead from anywhere in an organization. You can lead without a title. You can lead without formal authority. You can lead from the front line, the middle, or even from the outside.

And in the age of AI, when hierarchies flatten, when work becomes more project-based, when traditional command-and-control structures become obsolete, this kind of leadership at all levels becomes the only kind that matters.

WHY LEADERSHIP AT ALL LEVELS MATTERS MORE THAN EVER

Remember the 7-Sided Pincer Movement? ERP and SAP. White-collar robots. Globalization. Outsourcing. The internet. Disruptive competition. AI. Every one of those forces is eliminating routine work, flattening organizations, and accelerating change.

Ray Kurzweil, whose predictions have proven accurate at an 86% rate over three decades, has set 2029 as the year a machine will match and surpass human intelligence. Whether he is right by a year or five years, that window demands a different kind of leadership — not slower, more deliberate hierarchy, but faster, more distributed, human-centered leadership that AI cannot replicate and no algorithm can replace.

In the same week I completed this manuscript, 39 companies announced layoffs totaling more than 600,000 jobs. The CEO of Anthropic warned on national television that AI could spike unemployment 10 to 20 percent within five years. The organizations that will navigate that environment are not the ones with the best AI tools. They are the ones with the strongest leadership culture — people at every level who take ownership, drive solutions, and refuse to wait for someone else to act.

Command-and-control leadership does not work anymore. You cannot mandate innovation. You cannot order people to be engaged. You cannot force discretionary performance.

What works is creating a culture where people voluntarily choose to give their best work. Where they take ownership of problems without being told. Where they adapt to change instead of resisting it.

*When change happens every week instead of every year, you cannot wait for decisions to flow up and down a hierarchy.
You need people throughout the organization who can see what needs to happen and make it happen.*

That is leadership at all levels. And it is the fifth ingredient of your Kryptonite defense.

YOU ARE A LEADER

Let me be direct about something:

You are a leader. Right now. Today.

Not because of your title. Not because of who reports to you. You are a leader because you are the only person who will lead your life, your career, and your destiny.

Do not delegate that to somebody else. Do not wait for your boss to develop you. Do not assume your company will take care of you. Do not hope loyalty will be rewarded.

You must take accountability and ownership for where you are going and how you will get there.

That is leadership. And it starts with leading yourself.

But leadership does not stop there. Because every action you take creates an experience for others. Every decision you make influences people around you. Every problem you solve — or avoid solving — affects your team, your organization, your customers.

Whether you have a leadership title or not, you are leading. The only question is: Are you leading intentionally or accidentally? Are you creating the culture you want — or just reacting to the culture around you?

THE FIVE PRACTICES OF EXEMPLARY LEADERSHIP

I had the opportunity to work with Jim Kouzes early in my career. Jim spent 30 years researching exemplary leadership, conducting thousands of case studies to answer one question:

Why do people voluntarily choose to follow certain leaders?

Not why do they have to follow them. Why do they choose to.

After three decades of research, Kouzes and his partner Barry Posner identified five practices that exemplary leaders consistently demonstrate. And here is what matters: These practices do not require a title. They do not require formal authority. They require choice.

Practice 1: Model the Way

Set the example for others by behaving in ways that are consistent with your stated values. Achieve small wins that promote consistent progress and build commitment.

Do what you say you will do. Do not ever expect anybody else to do what you are not willing to do yourself.

"What you do speaks so loud I cannot hear what you say."
— Ralph Waldo Emerson

Remember the hand clap demonstration? I ask people to clap on three. I clap on two and a half. What do most people do? They follow my actions, not my words.

Words are cheap. People will tolerate what you say. They will ultimately act on what they see you do.

This is modeling the way. Your actions create experiences for everyone watching. Those experiences develop beliefs about what is acceptable, what is expected, what matters.

If you say we value work-life balance but send emails at 11 PM every night — what are you modeling?
If you say we embrace failure as learning but punish every mistake — what are you modeling?
If you say collaboration matters but hoard information — what are you modeling?

People do not follow what you say. They follow what you do.
Model the behavior you want to see.

The Power of Small Wins

Modeling the way also means achieving small wins that promote consistent progress and build commitment. You do not need to transform everything overnight. Small, visible wins build momentum. They prove that change is possible. They convert skeptics into believers.

Sarah did this. She did not try to fix the entire quality system in one meeting. She helped the team identify three bottlenecks and commit to testing two small changes. Those small wins created momentum for bigger changes.

Practice 2: Inspire Shared Vision

Envision an uplifting and ennobling future. Enlist others in a common vision by appealing to their values, interests, hopes and dreams.

Paint such a crystal clear vision of the future and what is possible that people will voluntarily choose to help you make it reality.

This is not about creating a fancy vision statement that sits on a wall. This is about helping people see what success looks like and why it matters — to them, to their team, to the company, to all stakeholders, to their community, to their families.

The most difficult challenge a leader will face is driving a strategy that requires other people to voluntarily choose to change their behavior. You cannot force people to change. You can only inspire them to choose change.

Great leaders make the future so tangible you can almost touch it. When people can see themselves in the vision — when they understand how achieving it benefits everyone — they stop doing the minimum required and start doing what is possible.

Four Critical Shifts That Create a Vision People Choose to Follow

POSSIBILITIES VS. TACTICS

Focus on what is possible, not just tactical execution. Paint the picture of what could be, not just what needs to be done next. Tactics tell people what to do. Possibilities inspire people to imagine. Tactics alone will never fully engage the heart, the passion, and the commitment.

WANT TO VS. HAVE TO

Create desire, not obligation. When people want to achieve something, they find ways. When they have to do something, they find excuses. The difference is whether they see the vision as their opportunity or your mandate.

PULL VS. PUSH

Attract people to the vision rather than forcing compliance. Pull creates momentum. Push creates resistance. When the vision is compelling enough, people pull themselves toward it. You do not have to push them.

FOCUS ON RESULTS VS. FOCUS ON ACTIVITY

Be outcome-oriented, not just focused on keeping busy. People want to know they are making progress toward something that matters, not just completing tasks. Results energize. Activity exhausts.

Urgency Before Strategy

Here is what most leaders get wrong: They work on strategy first because urgency is not easy. Most business leaders were trained in strategy, not in behavioral change. But strategy alone does not create adequate thrust and momentum.

Senior leaders often see the WHY in the strategy and the result. They believe it is apparent to everyone. The reality is this often is not the case. Before people can execute your strategy, they need to feel urgency about why change matters. Without urgency, even the best strategy sits on a shelf.

Sarah created urgency with a simple question: What if we could fix this together? That question made the problem and the opportunity feel immediate and personal.

Many of the insights I share about complacency, false urgency, and true urgency come from my years working alongside Dr. John Kotter at Kotter International, where we helped clients successfully implement his renowned 8-Step Process for Leading Change. Working directly with John deepened my understanding of why urgency must precede strategy — and how leaders at every level can distinguish between frantic activity and genuine momentum. In 27 years, I have watched organizations fail at transformation not because their strategy was wrong, but because they never created the true urgency required to make people choose to change.

Practice 3: Challenge the Process

Look at what you are doing. If you need to blow it up to get better, blow it up.

You cannot be complacent. You cannot maintain the status quo. The world is changing too fast. What worked last year may not work this year. What works today may not work next month.

Leaders challenge the process. They ask: Why do we do it this way? Is there a better approach? What are we missing? What would we do if we started from scratch today?

This does not mean changing things just to change them. It means being relentlessly curious about whether your current approach is still the best approach.

The Hidden Enemy: Complacency

The biggest barrier to challenging the process is complacency. And complacency is more pervasive than most leaders recognize. It is often invisible to insiders.

Complacency is rooted in past success — real or perceived wins. It creates a mindset of "I know what and how to do it." It makes employees content with the status quo and anxious about the unknown.

How does complacency manifest in organizations?

People defend the way things have always been done
New ideas get shot down with "That will never work here"
Teams resist even small experiments with different approaches
Success is defined by maintaining last year's performance
Nobody questions whether current processes still make sense

Complacency feels safe. But in a rapidly changing world, complacency is deadly. It is the reason Blockbuster missed streaming. It is the reason Kodak missed digital. It is the reason Nokia missed smartphones.

Challenging the process means challenging complacency. Constantly. Relentlessly. Even when — especially when — things are working well.

You Do Not Need Authority to Challenge the Process

You need courage. The courage to ask the hard questions. The courage to propose a different way. The courage to experiment and learn. The courage to say: I think there might be a better approach.

Sarah did not have authority over engineering or operations. But she had the courage to challenge the assumption that these groups could not work together. She challenged the process not by demanding change, but by creating an opportunity for people to see a different way forward.

Practice 4: Enable Others to Act

Build skills and abilities in others. Remove obstacles and barriers. Provide resources. Be available. Develop skills and competencies. Match skills with abilities.

This is not about doing the work for them. It is about clearing the path so they can do the work themselves.

What barriers are your people facing? Bureaucratic processes that slow them down? Lack of information they need? Missing tools or resources? Unclear priorities? Conflicting directives?

Leaders remove those obstacles. They ask: What is preventing you from being successful? Then they address it.

And they build capabilities in others. Not by telling them what to do, but by developing their judgment, their skills, their confidence. By giving them challenges that stretch them. By trusting them with meaningful work.

The Critical Distinction: False Urgency vs. True Urgency

One of the biggest mistakes leaders make when trying to enable others is creating false urgency instead of true urgency. And most do not realize they are doing it.

FALSE URGENCY: THE ACTIVITY TRAP

False urgency comes from failures, recent problems with short-term results, or long-standing incremental decline. It creates a mindset of "What a mess this is" or "We tried this in the past."

Employees operating under false urgency are often anxious, angry, frustrated, tired, and focused on activity to cover their concerns. The result is frenetic behavior: meeting after meeting, PowerPoint after PowerPoint, task force after task force. Lots of motion. Little progress. People are busy. Exhausted. But not productive.

TRUE URGENCY: THE RESULTS FOCUS

True urgency requires leadership up and down the organization who create true urgency and re-create it when needed. The mindset of true urgency is: Great opportunities and hazards are everywhere. It creates a powerful desire to move and win now.

People operating under true urgency come to work every day determined to exploit real opportunities and avoid real hazards. They are focused on results, not just activity.

What True Urgency Sounds Like

"I found two ways that I can be visible to my people today."
"I look for ways to say yes to all of my people who want to help our opportunity be successful."
"I know something I can do to move the needle forward."
"I am empowering others to do tasks I used to do so that I can focus on our opportunity."
"I am purging non-value-added activities out of my schedule."
"I love catching people in the act of helping change happen."
"It is not about what we cannot do. It is about what we can do."

Telltale Signs of Missing Urgency

Over-analyzing when speed is essential

Employees assigned to task forces to study strategy — not execute it

No bias for action, just endless discussion

Meetings conclude with no decisions about immediate next steps

People blaming others for lack of progress

Specific assignments regularly not completed on time

Schedules too full to attend important meetings

Four Tactics to Increase True Urgency

Bring the Outside In. Reconnect internal reality with external opportunities and hazards. Bring in emotionally compelling data, people, video, imagery, sites and sounds. Make the external reality tangible and impossible to ignore.

Behave with Urgency Every Day. Never act content, anxious, or angry. Demonstrate your own sense of urgency in all that you do. Your behavior creates the experience that shapes beliefs about whether urgency matters here.

Find Opportunity in Crises. Always be alert to see if crises can be a friend, not just a dreadful enemy, in order to destroy complacency. Proceed with caution and never be naive — but used wisely, crises create urgency that complacency cannot survive.

Deal with the No-Nos and Naysayers. Remove or neutralize the relentless urgency killers and those determined to maintain the status quo. You cannot let urgency killers poison the environment.

Practice 5: Encourage the Heart

It is okay to have fun. People need to know they are winning. Celebrate progress. Recognize contributions. Show appreciation.

The deepest principle of human nature is a craving to be appreciated.

This is not just a nice sentiment. It is a fundamental truth about human motivation. One of the deepest cravings a human being has is the need to feel appreciated. Not just compensated. Appreciated. Seen. Valued. Recognized.

Most organizations are pretty good at pointing out what is wrong. They are terrible at celebrating what is right.

Preventing the Decline: Three Stages Leaders Must Watch

Why does encouraging the heart matter so much? Because without it, morale follows a predictable decline:

Stage 1: The Questioning Phase. People start asking themselves the hard questions: "Is this actually going anywhere? Are we just spinning our wheels? Does anybody upstairs even see what we're doing down here?" They're still in the game, still contributing — but seeds of doubt are taking root. This is your early warning signal.

Stage 2: The Belief Collapse. Now doubt hardens into disbelief. People stop believing anything will actually change. They stop trusting that leadership means what they say. They stop volunteering for the tough assignments. This is where you're losing them — and most leaders don't even realize it's happening.

Stage 3: The Mental Checkout. They're done. They show up physically but they're gone mentally. They do exactly what's required and not one thing more. Here's the brutal truth: once people reach this stage, getting them back is nearly impossible. You haven't just lost their discretionary effort. You've lost their hearts.

Encouraging the heart prevents this decline.
When people feel appreciated, when progress is celebrated,
when wins are recognized, they stay in the game.
They keep believing. They keep trying.

Without Ceremonies, There Are No Beginnings, No Endings

This is why celebration matters. Ceremonies mark progress. They create moments that people remember. They signal: Something important happened here. We achieved something worth acknowledging.

It does not have to be elaborate. Sarah did not throw a big party when her team reduced quality issues by 40%. But she did bring pizza again and say: Look at what you accomplished. This is proof that when we work together, we can solve anything.

That moment mattered. It encouraged hearts. It built belief.
It created momentum.

You Do Not Need Authority to Encourage the Heart

You can tell a colleague: That was a great idea in the meeting. You can tell your boss: I really appreciate how you handled that situation. You can tell your team: We are making progress and I am proud to work with all of you.

Recognition from peers is sometimes more powerful than recognition from bosses because it is freely given, not obligatory. When you generously recognize others, you build culture.

These five practices are not complicated. But they are powerful. And they work whether you are a CEO or a front-line employee. Because leadership is not about authority. Leadership is about the experiences you create and the culture you cultivate.

THE CULTURE YOU CREATE

Let me tell you something that most leaders miss:

Your job is not to manage tasks or control processes or enforce policies. Your job is to cultivate culture.

Because culture is what produces every result you achieve. Your financial results. Your operational results. Your customer results. Your employee results. All of them come from your culture.

And what is culture? Culture is how people think and act.

That is it. Not complicated. Your culture is the bottom three layers of the Results Model:

EXPERIENCES → BELIEFS → ACTIONS → RESULTS

Culture is the beliefs and actions part. How your people think and what they do. If you want to change your results, you cannot just change the actions people take. You have to change the beliefs that drive those actions. And to change beliefs, you have to create new experiences.

This is why leadership at all levels matters. Because everyone in your organization is creating experiences for others. Those experiences shape beliefs. Those beliefs drive actions. Those actions produce your results.

A Culture Example

Think about a team where people show up late to meetings, multitask through presentations, and rarely follow through on commitments.

What is the belief driving that action? Probably something like: This meeting does not really matter. My time is more valuable than this. Nobody holds anyone accountable anyway.

Where did that belief come from? Experiences. Someone showed up late once and nothing happened. Someone multitasked and nobody said anything. Someone missed a deadline and faced no consequences.

Those experiences created a belief. That belief drives actions. Those actions produce the result of an ineffective, disengaged team.

Your job as a leader at any level is to create the experiences that develop the beliefs that drive the actions that produce the results you want.

CULTIVATING A CULTURE OF ACCOUNTABILITY

The most effective, peak-performing culture you can create is a culture of accountability.

Not accountability as blame. Not accountability as punishment. Accountability as ownership. As people choosing to take responsibility for results — to solve problems proactively, to ask "what else can I do" instead of "that is not my job."

I wrote an entire book on this topic, Achieve with Accountability, so I am not going to recreate that work here. But I want to give you the framework that matters most for leadership in the age of AI.

Accountability is a journey with four keys. You cannot skip steps. You have to move through all four to truly take accountability.

Key 1: Recognize Realities

You cannot solve a problem you do not see or will not acknowledge. The first key is seeing reality as it is, not as you wish it were.

This requires open and candid communication. Being open to perspectives of others. Asking for and offering feedback. Talking about the elephant in the room. Anticipating opportunities and threats.

I use a demonstration in my keynotes that makes this undeniable. I flash a collage on a screen — thirty different objects. The audience has four seconds to memorize as many as they can. Four seconds. Thirty objects. Go.

Then I ask: What did you see? And the answers come fast. A panda bear. A baby. Pizza. Coke. A cruise ship. A guitar. Chopsticks. A car. Toblerone chocolate. Each person locks in on something different.

But here is where it gets real. I ask the room: Why did you see what you saw?

Some people saw things that were familiar to them. Colors drew others in. Some lingered on certain objects longer. And here is one that stops people cold — where you were seated in the room impacted what you saw. Your physical position changed your perception. Just as where you are seated in your organization impacts the way you see the operation.

Then I ask: Did anyone identify all thirty? Not one person. Not ever. But if we kept going, pooling every answer in the room, we would get them all.

And then I throw one more question at them. Nobody mentioned the carry-on bag. What if that carry-on bag was a huge opportunity and we missed it? We missed it because there was no open and candid conversation. No one asked. No one offered a perspective. And we walked right past it. Now flip it — what if that carry-on bag was a huge hazard?

Seeing reality has more to do with our ears than it does with our eyes. A single perspective is the enemy of reality.

Key 2: Accept Ownership

Once you see reality, you have to own your part in creating it. Even if you did not cause the problem, you have to own your role in solving it.

This is not about blame. This is about recognizing: What have I done and not done to contribute to this situation? What is my responsibility here?

The opposite of ownership is the blame game. Pointing fingers. Making excuses. Saying it is not my fault, there is nothing I can do.

Leaders accept ownership. They say: This is my responsibility.
I may not control everything, but I control my response.
I may not have created this mess, but I will help clean it up.

Key 3: Create Solutions

Accountability is not just confession. It is action. Once you recognize reality and accept ownership, you have to create a solution.

This is where most people stop. They see the problem. They admit their part. But then they wait for someone else to fix it.

Leaders ask: What else can I do? That is the solve-it question.
Not what can I do if conditions were perfect. Not what could

I do if I had more resources. What else can I do right now with what I have?

There is always something. Always. Even if it is small. Even if it is imperfect. There is always a next step you can take.

Key 4: Exercise Action

Solutions without execution are just ideas. The fourth key is taking action. Actually doing what you said you would do.

This completes the accountability loop. You see reality. You own your part. You create a solution. You execute.

And then you start the loop again. Because taking action creates new realities that you have to recognize, own, solve, and act on.

Accountability is not a one-time thing. It is a continuous cycle. And organizations that build this into their culture — where people at all levels consistently move through these four keys — those organizations are unstoppable.

LEADERSHIP RADAR: THE FOUR-LAYER ADVANTAGE

Here is what separates good leaders from great ones:

Great leaders operate with what I call Leadership Radar. They understand what is in the heart and head of the people they work with and lead.

Two-Layer Thinkers vs. Four-Layer Thinkers

Most people operate with a two-layer model:

ACTIONS → RESULTS

They see what people do and they see the results those actions produce. When results are not what they want, they focus on changing actions — tell people what to do differently, enforce compliance, direct, mandate, control.

This is exhausting. It is energy-draining and time-consuming. And it does not work sustainably because when you are not watching, people revert back to their beliefs and take action accordingly.

Great leaders operate with a four-layer model:

EXPERIENCES → BELIEFS → ACTIONS → RESULTS

They understand that actions come from beliefs. And beliefs come from experiences. So if you want to change actions, you cannot just tell people to do something different. You have to understand why they believe what they believe. And if you want to change beliefs, you have to create new experiences.

The Difference in Action

Two-layer thinker sees: Team member is not speaking up in meetings.

Two-layer response: Tell them to contribute more. Maybe give them a task to present next meeting.

Result: They present when required but still do not volunteer ideas. No real change.

Four-layer thinker sees the same thing but asks different questions:

What is the action? Not speaking up.

What is the belief driving that action? Probably: "My ideas are not valued" or "When I speak up I get shot down" or "It is safer to stay quiet."

What experiences created that belief? Maybe they shared an idea once and got dismissed. Maybe nobody ever asked for their input.

Four-layer response: Create new experiences. Ask them directly for input. When they share, build on it publicly. Recognize their contribution afterward — privately and publicly.

Over time, new experiences create a new belief. That new belief drives new action. This is Leadership Radar.

Why This Builds Trust

People who operate with four-layer thinking are viewed with high levels of trust. Because they demonstrate understanding. They recognize that people are not just acting randomly — they are acting based on beliefs. And those beliefs make sense given the experiences people have had.

Four-layer thinkers do not judge or dismiss. They seek to understand. And when people feel understood, they trust you.

Leadership Radar is the difference. And it is available to anyone who chooses to operate with all four layers of the Results Model.

LEADING WITHOUT AUTHORITY

Let us come back to Sarah from the beginning of this chapter.

She had no formal authority. No direct reports. No budget. No official mandate to solve the quality problem.

But she led anyway. And she achieved results that executives with far more authority had failed to achieve.

Authority is about compliance. Leadership is about influence. Authority can make people do things. Leadership makes people want to do things.

And in the age of AI, when work becomes more collaborative, more project-based, more fluid — the ability to lead without authority becomes the most valuable skill you can develop.

How to Lead Through Influence

Model the Behavior You Want to See

You do not need a title to demonstrate accountability, ownership, excellence, or collaboration. When you consistently model the behaviors your team needs, others notice. Your actions create experiences. Those experiences shape beliefs about what is normal here.

Sarah modeled curiosity. She modeled collaboration. She modeled ownership. Others followed that example.

Ask Powerful Questions

You do not need authority to ask: What if we tried this? How could we make this better? What would you do if there were no constraints? Great questions create thinking. Thinking creates engagement. Engagement leads to action.

Sarah asked: What if we could fix this together? That question unlocked collaboration that formal mandates had failed to create.

Create Clarity Around What Matters

Most people are not lazy or incompetent. They are unclear. They do not know what success looks like or how their work contributes.

When you help people see: This is what we are trying to achieve, this is why it matters, this is how your work connects to that goal — you create clarity. Clarity creates focus. Focus creates results. You do not need authority to clarify. You just need to care enough to help people understand.

Remove Obstacles

When you see something blocking progress, address it. Do not wait for permission. If you cannot remove it yourself, escalate it. Bring it to someone who can.

Leaders who enable others to act are valued whether they have authority or not. Because they make other people's work easier.

Recognize Contributions

You do not need a title to say: Great idea. That really helped. I learned something from how you handled that.

Recognition from peers is often more meaningful than recognition from bosses because it is freely given, not obligatory. When you generously recognize others, you build influence.

Invite People Into Solution-Finding

Instead of complaining about problems, invite others to solve them with you. "I am working on this challenge. Would you brainstorm with me?"

This creates ownership without requiring authority. Because when people co-create solutions, they own the outcome.

THE ONE THING AI WILL NEVER DO

AI can analyze data. AI can optimize processes. AI can automate tasks. AI can even make recommendations.

But AI cannot lead.

AI cannot inspire a shared vision. AI cannot model the way. AI cannot encourage the heart. AI cannot create the experiences that develop beliefs that drive discretionary performance.

AI cannot cultivate culture.

This is why leadership at all levels is the fifth ingredient of your Kryptonite defense. Because it is the one ingredient AI will never replicate.

And the beautiful thing about leadership? It is accessible to everyone.

You do not need a title. You do not need formal authority. You do not need permission.

You just need to choose to lead.

SARAH CHOSE TO LEAD

Six months after that initial lunch, the plant manager promoted Sarah. Not because she had asked for it. Not because she had lobbied for it. But because she had demonstrated leadership.

She had created a culture where people solved problems collaboratively instead of blaming each other. She had modeled accountability. She had enabled others to act. She had challenged processes that were not working.

She led. And leadership creates opportunity.

But here is what matters most: Sarah did not wait for a title to lead. She did not wait for authority. She did not wait for permission. She saw what needed to happen. And she made it happen.

That is leadership. And it is available to you right now. Today. In whatever role you currently have.

LEADERSHIP IS YOUR CHOICE

Leadership is not something that happens to you when you get promoted. Leadership is something you choose to practice every day.

You choose to model the behavior you want to see instead of complaining about what others do.

You choose to inspire vision instead of just completing tasks.

You choose to challenge processes that are not working instead of accepting the status quo.

You choose to enable others instead of hoarding information or resources.

You choose to encourage and recognize instead of only pointing out problems.

You choose to cultivate culture through the experiences you create.

You choose to take accountability instead of playing the blame game.

You choose to operate with Leadership Radar — understanding what people believe and why, and creating the experiences that develop the beliefs you want.

You choose to lead through influence, even when you have no authority.

These are all choices. And these choices, accumulated day after day, interaction after interaction, create your impact as a leader.

LEADERSHIP AT ALL LEVELS: THE FIFTH INGREDIENT OF YOUR KRYPTONITE DEFENSE

You have built your ideas muscle. You have developed speed. You have multiplied talent. You have created distinction.

Now you have the fifth ingredient: Leadership at all levels.

This is what ties everything together. Because without leadership, ideas remain just ideas. Speed creates chaos instead of progress. Talent sits dormant instead of multiplying. Distinction fades instead of growing.

Leadership is what activates everything else. It is what transforms individual capabilities into collective impact. It is what builds cultures where people voluntarily give their best work.

And in the age of AI, when the 7-Sided Pincer Movement threatens to displace tens of millions of workers, when automation eliminates routine work, when technical skills become commoditized — leadership becomes your ultimate competitive advantage.

Because AI will never replace the human ability to inspire, to connect, to create meaning, to cultivate culture, to make people feel valued and motivated to contribute.

AI will never replace leadership.

So lead. Not someday when you get the right title. Not eventually when conditions are perfect. Now. From wherever you are.

Because the world needs leaders at all levels. Your organization needs it. Your team needs it. Your career depends on it.

And your choice to lead — right now, today — might be exactly what makes you indispensable in the age of AI.

Those prepared need not fear the forces at work.

. . .

COMING UP: PUTTING IT ALL TOGETHER

You now have all five ingredients of your Kryptonite defense:

IDEAS — Your ability to generate and implement breakthrough thinking
SPEED — Your capacity to move faster than the pace of change
TALENT — Your skill at multiplying capabilities in yourself and others
DISTINCTION — Your commitment to being memorably valuable
LEADERSHIP — Your choice to create culture and drive results at all levels

In the chapter ahead, we will explore how to integrate these ingredients, how to deploy them strategically, and how to make yourself truly future-proof in an age where AI is rewriting every rule of work.

The 7-Sided Pincer Movement is real. The threat is urgent. But you now have the defense. The question is: Will you use it?

INTEGRATION

*Putting Your Kryptonite
Defense Together*

"I HAD ALL THE PIECES"

"I had all the pieces," Marcus said, staring at the severance agreement on his desk. "I just never put them together."

Five months earlier, Marcus had attended my keynote at a regional insurance conference. He didn't tell me which company he worked for. He didn't ask for a business card. He just cornered me afterward in the hallway, eyes bright with energy, talking a mile a minute about how everything I'd said about the 7-Sided Pincer Movement made perfect sense.

"Mike, this is exactly what we need! I'm going to implement everything: new ideas, faster processes, better talent development, distinction in the market, leadership at all levels. All of it!"

I remember thinking: This guy gets it. He understood the threat. He saw the urgency. He had the passion.

I never heard from him again.

Until five months later, when he called asking if we could talk.

Over those five months, Marcus had launched initiatives across all five Kryptonite ingredients:

He created an innovation lab (IDEAS)
He mandated faster approval cycles (SPEED)
He hired three new team members with AI skills (TALENT)
He rebranded his division with a new tagline (DISTINCTION)
He enrolled his managers in a leadership course (LEADERSHIP)

When we finally spoke, Marcus walked me through everything he'd done. On paper, it looked impressive. Five major initiatives. Significant investment. Measurable activity.

But as he talked, I started asking questions:

"Did the innovation lab work with the people you hired who had AI skills?"

"No, different departments."

"Did the faster approval process apply to the ideas from the innovation lab?"

"No, that was for operational decisions, not innovation."

"Did the rebranding effort highlight the new capabilities from your AI hires?"

"Not really. Marketing ran the rebrand. IT ran the AI hiring."

"Did your leadership training teach managers how to drive innovation or speed?"

"It was general leadership development. Good stuff, but not specific to those initiatives."

The pattern became clear. Marcus had launched five separate initiatives. But he never connected them.

He never connected the innovation lab to the faster approval process, so great ideas died in bureaucracy. He never aligned the new AI talent with the rebranding effort, so distinction remained superficial. He never equipped his managers to lead the innovation or speed initiatives, so leadership training felt theoretical.

Each ingredient existed in isolation. The innovation lab generated ideas that the approval process killed. The talented new hires worked on projects disconnected from market distinction. The leadership training had no practical application.

Meanwhile, a much smaller competitor, a company I had been working with dating back to my time at Kotter International and Tom Peters Company, integrated their approach. They used AI talent to accelerate their approval process, which enabled rapid innovation, which created genuine market distinction, which their leaders championed with urgency. I had watched that pattern work inside Fortune 50 companies for 27 years. Isolated initiatives rarely compound. Integrated systems almost always do.

Six months after that keynote, Marcus was out. The competitor had won the business of three of his largest clients.

"I had all the pieces," Marcus repeated.
"I just thought having them was enough."

THE FATAL FLAW OF FRAGMENTED EXCELLENCE

Marcus made the mistake that dooms most transformation efforts. He treated the five Kryptonite ingredients as a checklist rather than a system.

CHECK: IDEAS ✓ SPEED ✓ TALENT ✓ DISTINCTION ✓ LEADERSHIP ✓

But having the ingredients doesn't mean you're cooking a meal. You can have flour, eggs, sugar, butter, and vanilla sitting on your counter, but until you combine them properly and apply heat, you don't have a cake. You just have ingredients.

We've spent considerable time exploring each ingredient of your Kryptonite defense:

IDEAS — How to innovate constantly in a world where AI out-executes humans

SPEED — How to move faster than disruption can disrupt you

TALENT — How to develop capabilities that AI can't replicate

DISTINCTION — How to create The Big 3 that makes you irreplaceable

LEADERSHIP — How to lead change at every level, not just from the top

> *But if you treat these as five separate initiatives, you'll end up like Marcus, busy, well-intentioned, and ultimately displaced. Integration isn't the sixth ingredient. Integration is what transforms five good ideas into an unstoppable defense.*

WHY INTEGRATION MULTIPLIES — NOT JUST ADDS

A few years ago, I was having lunch with a friend, an MIT graduate and one of the smartest people I know. I was telling him about organizations that implement the five Kryptonite ingredients but still fail.

"They do everything I tell them," I said, frustrated. "They innovate. They move fast. They develop talent. They create distinction. They lead. But somehow, they're still getting beat by competitors who seem less prepared."

My friend grabbed a napkin and pulled out a pen.

"Mike, you're thinking about this wrong. Let me show you the math."

And right there, over lunch, he showed me something that changed how I think about transformation.

THE NAPKIN MATH

If you score 5 out of 10 on each of the five Kryptonite ingredients and you simply add them together, your total score is 25 out of 50. That sounds pretty good. 50% proficiency across all five areas. Not great, but survivable, right?

Wrong.

"The problem," my friend said, "is that these ingredients don't add. They multiply."

$$5 \times 5 \times 5 \times 5 \times 5 = 3{,}125 \text{ OUT OF } 100{,}000$$

That's 3% effectiveness. Mediocrity across all five areas doesn't give you a passing grade. It gives you extinction.

Then he showed me what happens when you integrate the ingredients and improve each one to just 7 out of 10:

$$7 \times 7 \times 7 \times 7 \times 7 = 16{,}807 \text{ OUT OF } 100{,}000$$

"That's a 438% improvement," he said, "and you only improved each ingredient by 40%."

Then he wrote one more calculation:

$$8 \times 8 \times 8 \times 8 \times 8 = 32{,}768 \text{ OUT OF } 100{,}000$$

"That's 10 times more effective than the 5/10 approach."

I kept that napkin. It's framed in my office.

And this is not abstract math. Organizations that fragmented their AI efforts in 2023 and 2024, launching isolated initiatives rather than integrated systems, now face competitors carrying more than 18 months of compounding advantage. That gap is the multiplication principle made real. Fragmented effort doesn't just underperform integrated effort. It falls exponentially further behind with every passing quarter. The 600,000 layoffs announced in a single week as I completed this manuscript were not random. They were concentrated in organizations that had isolated their AI adoption, treating it as a technology initiative rather than an integrated business transformation.

Small improvements across an integrated system create exponential results. Fragmented excellence creates linear mediocrity.

THE INTEGRATION MATRIX: HOW THE INGREDIENTS AMPLIFY EACH OTHER

Let me show you exactly how the five Kryptonite ingredients work together. This isn't theory. This is the practical reality of how future-proof people and organizations operate.

IDEAS + SPEED = INNOVATION THAT ACTUALLY SHIPS

Ideas without speed die in committees. Speed without ideas is just frantic activity. But when you combine them:

Your innovation lab has a 48-hour decision rule
Prototypes get tested with customers in days, not months
Failed experiments are killed quickly, freeing resources for better ideas
Your team develops "ship it or kill it" muscle memory

Amazon's "two-pizza team" rule combines IDEAS (small teams innovate better) with SPEED (small teams move faster). The result? They launch more new products than any company in history.

IDEAS + TALENT = INNOVATION THAT'S ACTUALLY POSSIBLE

Ideas without talent are fantasy. Talent without ideas is wasted potential. But when you combine them:

Your team develops skills specifically aligned with strategic priorities
Innovation challenges become talent development opportunities
People see how learning directly enables execution
Your best ideas are pursued by people capable of delivering them

Apple doesn't just generate great product ideas.
They develop design and engineering talent specifically to execute those ideas. The integration of IDEAS + TALENT is why Apple products actually ship at the quality level they envision.

IDEAS + DISTINCTION = INNOVATION THAT MATTERS TO CUSTOMERS

Ideas without distinction are me-too products. Distinction without ideas is hollow branding. But when you combine them:

Every innovation is filtered through The Big 3: Is it dramatically different? Does it deliver overt benefit? Can we prove it?
You innovate where competitors can't or won't follow
Customers immediately understand why your solution is unique
Your ideas create separation, not just incremental improvement

Tesla didn't just build electric cars (IDEAS). They built the fastest, longest-range, most technologically advanced cars that happened to be electric (DISTINCTION). The integration made them the most valuable car company in the world.

SPEED + TALENT = EXECUTION THAT COMPOUNDS

Speed without talent creates rework. Talent without speed creates missed opportunities. But when you combine them:

Your team gets faster AND better with each cycle
Learning happens in real-time through rapid execution
Skills develop through doing, not just training
Experience compounds faster than competitors

SpaceX combines SPEED (rapid launch cadence) with TALENT (engineers who learn from each launch). The result? They went from zero to dominating the space launch industry in a decade.

SPEED + DISTINCTION = FIRST-MOVER ADVANTAGE THAT LASTS

Speed without distinction means you're fast to mediocre. Distinction without speed means competitors copy you before you scale. But when you combine them:

You establish market position before competitors react
Your distinctiveness compounds as you iterate faster
Customers associate your brand with innovation leadership
Competitors chase yesterday's version of your offering

Netflix combined SPEED (pivoting from DVDs to streaming to original content) with DISTINCTION (personalization algorithms, binge-release model). Each fast move created new separation from competitors.

TALENT + DISTINCTION = THE CAPABILITIES THAT MATTER MOST

Talent without distinction is generic skill development. Distinction without talent is a promise you can't keep. But when you combine them:

You develop exactly the capabilities that deliver your unique value
Your talent development reinforces what makes you different
Customers experience the expertise that backs your brand promise
Your people become as distinctive as your offerings

*Ritz-Carlton combines TALENT (legendary service training) with
DISTINCTION ("Ladies and Gentlemen serving Ladies
and Gentlemen"). Every employee embodies the brand's unique
positioning.*

LEADERSHIP = THE INGREDIENT THAT ACTIVATES EVERYTHING ELSE

Leadership without the other four ingredients is inspiration without execution. The other four without leadership is potential without direction. But when you integrate LEADERSHIP with everything else:

IDEAS — Leaders create the conditions where innovation thrives
SPEED — Leaders remove obstacles and make fast decisions
TALENT — Leaders develop people as a daily discipline
DISTINCTION — Leaders champion what makes the organization unique
Plus: Leaders model the integration itself

*Leadership is the catalytic ingredient. It doesn't replace
the other four. It activates them, connects them, and ensures
they work as a system rather than as isolated initiatives.*

INTEGRATION IN ACTION: THREE REAL-WORLD EXAMPLES

EXAMPLE 1: THE HOSPITAL THAT BECAME AI-PROOF

Cleveland Clinic didn't just adopt AI tools (IDEAS). They:

Trained every physician and nurse in AI literacy (TALENT)
Reduced diagnostic turnaround time from days to hours (SPEED)
Created a distinctive patient experience combining human empathy with AI precision (DISTINCTION)
Empowered frontline staff to suggest AI applications (LEADERSHIP)

The result? AI made them more human, not less.
Patient satisfaction scores increased even as efficiency improved.
They attracted top talent specifically because of their
integrated approach.

EXAMPLE 2: THE SALES TEAM THAT THRIVED IN THE AI ERA

When Salesforce rolled out AI sales tools, most teams used them to automate tasks. One team leader integrated differently:

Used AI to handle routine follow-ups (SPEED)
Trained team on asking better questions AI couldn't answer (TALENT)
Positioned team as "AI-augmented advisors" not "AI-replaced salespeople" (DISTINCTION)
Let reps customize their AI workflows (IDEAS from the team)
Celebrated the reps who best combined AI speed with human insight (LEADERSHIP)

That team doubled revenue while competitors' teams were cut
by 30%. Same AI tools. Integrated approach.

EXAMPLE 3: THE MARKETING PROFESSIONAL WHO FUTURE-PROOFED HER CAREER

Sarah, a marketing director, watched AI tools threaten her team. Instead of resisting:

She learned six AI marketing tools in 90 days (TALENT + SPEED)
Used them to test 10X more campaign concepts (IDEAS)
Positioned herself as "AI-enabled strategist" internally and externally (DISTINCTION)
Trained her team on the tools, creating a leadership reputation (LEADERSHIP)
Delivered campaigns 50% faster at 30% lower cost while improving results

Two years later, she's VP of Marketing. Her former peers who dismissed AI tools are looking for jobs.

THE VIRTUOUS CYCLE: HOW INTEGRATION BECOMES UNSTOPPABLE

Here's the beautiful thing about integration: once you start, it accelerates on its own.

Better IDEAS attract better TALENT, which enables faster SPEED, which creates stronger DISTINCTION, which attracts more LEADERSHIP attention and resources, which funds more IDEAS, which develops more TALENT, which increases SPEED, which amplifies DISTINCTION, which demonstrates better LEADERSHIP...

It becomes a virtuous cycle that compounds over time.

Meanwhile, competitors stuck in fragmented excellence experience the opposite: a vicious cycle where mediocre IDEAS fail to attract TALENT, slow SPEED undermines DISTINCTION, weak DISTINCTION gets ignored by LEADERSHIP, lack of LEADERSHIP investment starves IDEAS…

The gap widens exponentially.

This is why you see companies like Apple, Amazon, Tesla, and Netflix pull so far ahead of competitors. It's not that they're 10% better at one thing, they're integrated, and integration compounds.

YOUR PERSONAL KRYPTONITE SCORECARD

Now it's time to assess where you stand, not just on each ingredient individually, but on integration itself.

Rate yourself honestly on a scale of 1-10 for each statement:

1 = STRONGLY DISAGREE | 10 = STRONGLY AGREE

IDEAS ASSESSMENT

___ I consistently generate new ideas relevant to my role

___ My ideas are welcomed and seriously considered

___ I test ideas quickly rather than over-analyzing

___ I learn from failed experiments without penalty

___ **IDEAS INTEGRATION:** My innovation efforts directly connect to speed, talent, distinction, and leadership initiatives

IDEAS TOTAL: ___ / 50

SPEED ASSESSMENT

___ I make decisions quickly without unnecessary delay

___ I eliminate bureaucracy and obstacles proactively

___ I ship work products fast and iterate based on feedback

___ I help others move faster, not slow them down

___ **SPEED INTEGRATION:** My speed initiatives directly support innovation, talent development, distinction, and leadership

SPEED TOTAL: ___ / 50

TALENT ASSESSMENT

___ I actively develop new skills and capabilities

___ I seek diverse perspectives and welcome disagreement

___ I learn continuously from every experience

___ I help develop others' capabilities

___ **TALENT INTEGRATION:** My learning directly enables me to innovate faster, create distinction, and lead effectively

TALENT TOTAL: ___ / 50

DISTINCTION ASSESSMENT

___ I can clearly articulate how I'm dramatically different from others in my role

___ I deliver overt benefits that people immediately recognize

___ I can prove my value with specific evidence

___ Others describe me using unique descriptors, not generic terms

____ **DISTINCTION INTEGRATION:** My unique value proposition is powered by innovation, speed, talent development, and leadership

DISTINCTION TOTAL: ____ / 50

LEADERSHIP ASSESSMENT

____ I lead change regardless of my title or position

____ I create urgency around what matters most

____ I champion initiatives that benefit others, not just myself

____ I model the behaviors I want to see in others

____ **LEADERSHIP INTEGRATION:** My leadership directly drives innovation, speed, talent development, and distinction across my sphere of influence

LEADERSHIP TOTAL: ____ / 50

INTERPRETING YOUR SCORECARD

Add your five totals together for your overall Kryptonite Score (Maximum: 250):

TOTAL SCORE: ____ / 250

But here's the critical question: Look at your fifth statement in each section — the INTEGRATION statements. Add those five scores together:

INTEGRATION SCORE: ____ / 50

This number tells you whether you're building a system or just collecting ingredients.

Integration score below 35: You're at risk of Marcus's fate — having the pieces but not putting them together.

Integration score 35–45: You're making connections but still operating somewhat in silos.

Integration score 45–50: You're thinking and acting systemically. You understand that the whole is greater than the sum of the parts.

WHERE TO START: YOUR 90-DAY INTEGRATION ACTION PLAN

Integration doesn't happen accidentally. It requires intentional design.

DAYS 1–30: MAP YOUR CURRENT STATE

Identify your current initiatives across all five ingredients

Map the connections — or lack thereof — between them

Find the biggest disconnects (where ingredients work against each other)

Prioritize the one integration that would create the most immediate value

DAYS 31–60: CREATE ONE INTEGRATION WIN

Pick TWO ingredients that aren't currently connected

Design one initiative that leverages both simultaneously

Launch it, learn from it, adjust quickly

Document the results and share the learning

Examples:

Connect IDEAS + SPEED by creating a "48-hour decision rule" for any innovation under $10K

Connect TALENT + DISTINCTION by training your team on the exact skills that deliver your unique value proposition

DAYS 61–90: SCALE THE INTEGRATION MODEL

Apply the integration approach to a second pair of ingredients
Look for "triple integrations" — three ingredients working together
Train others on integration thinking
Make integration a standard operating question: "How does this connect to our other initiatives?"

THE INTEGRATION MINDSET: THINKING LIKE A SYSTEMS ARCHITECT

Integration isn't just about connecting dots. It's about developing a different way of thinking.

Before making any decision, ask these five integration questions:

1. How does this generate or enable new IDEAS?
2. How does this increase our SPEED?
3. How does this develop TALENT?
4. How does this strengthen our DISTINCTION?
5. How does this demonstrate or develop LEADERSHIP?

If your initiative only addresses one ingredient, it's fragmented. If it addresses two or three, it's integrated. If it addresses four or five, it's transformational.

This is how you shift from doing five things adequately to building one integrated system that compounds over time.

KEY LEARNINGS: INTEGRATION

1. The five Kryptonite ingredients multiply, they don't add, mediocrity across all five equals extinction.

2. Integration transforms five good initiatives into an exponential defense against AI disruption.
3. IDEAS + SPEED = innovation that ships | IDEAS + TALENT = innovation that's possible | IDEAS + DISTINCTION = innovation that matters.
4. SPEED + TALENT = execution that compounds | SPEED + DISTINCTION = first-mover advantage | TALENT + DISTINCTION = capabilities that matter most.
5. LEADERSHIP activates and connects all four other ingredients.
6. Integration creates a virtuous cycle that accelerates over time.
7. Your integration score matters more than your individual ingredient scores.
8. Integration requires intentional design, not accidental coordination.
9. Before any initiative: ask how it connects to all five ingredients.
10. Small improvements across an integrated system create exponential results.

THE INTEGRATION IMPERATIVE

Marcus had all the pieces. You now have all the pieces too.

The question isn't whether you understand IDEAS, SPEED, TALENT, DISTINCTION, and LEADERSHIP individually. By now, you do.

The question is whether you'll treat them as a checklist or as a system.

In the age of AI, fragmented excellence is a death sentence. Integrated competence is a survival strategy. Integrated excellence is a competitive weapon.

You don't need to be perfect at all five ingredients. You need to be intentional about connecting them.

Because when you do, something remarkable happens:

$$5 \times 5 \times 5 \times 5 \times 5 = 3{,}125 \quad \text{(FRAGMENTED MEDIOCRITY)}$$

$$8 \times 8 \times 8 \times 8 \times 8 = 32{,}768 \quad \text{(INTEGRATED COMPETENCE)}$$

That's not just 10X better. That's the difference between distinct and extinct.

So here's your challenge: Over the next 90 days, identify one place where you'll connect two ingredients that are currently operating independently. Launch it. Learn from it. Then do it again.

Build the integration muscle. Develop the systems thinking. Create the virtuous cycle.

AI will displace the fragmented.
But it will amplify the integrated.
Those prepared need not fear the forces at work.

. . .

What Integration Actually Looks Like

I worked with a Fortune 500 company that was bleeding market share, struggling to attract talent, and watching competitors commoditize their core offerings. They had smart people. They had strong capabilities in pockets. But nothing was working together.

Five ingredients. All present. Zero integration.

What Integration Actually Looks Like

I worked with a Fortune 500 company that was bleeding market share, struggling to attract talent, and watching competitors commoditize their core offerings. They had smart people. They had strong capabilities in pockets. But nothing was working together.

Their IDEAS team was brilliant at innovation but operated in isolation. Their SPEED initiatives created chaos without direction. TALENT development existed but wasn't connected to business priorities. DISTINCTION efforts focused on marketing slogans rather than operational reality. And LEADERSHIP was concentrated at the top while the organization waited for direction.

Five ingredients. All present. Zero integration.

Here's what changed when they embraced the full Kryptonite framework:

From Reactive to Market-Shaping

Product development cycles that once took 18-24 months dropped to 6-9 months. But the transformation wasn't about speed alone. It was about IDEAS (innovation) × SPEED (rapid deployment) × TALENT (adaptive teams) working together. They moved from reacting to competitors to shaping market expectations.

From Compliance to Ownership

The cultural shift was visible within 90 days. Employees stopped asking "What am I supposed to do?" and started asking "What result are we trying to achieve?" This wasn't a training program. It was LEADERSHIP AT ALL LEVELS (distributed ownership) × TALENT (accountability and judgment) × IDEAS (problem-solving) integrating into daily work.

People became CEOs of their own contribution.

From Surviving to Dominating

Within 18 months, they weren't just surviving disruption. They were using it to pull away from competitors. Their Integration

Score, the measure of how well the five ingredients work together, went from 12 to 38. Not because any single ingredient was perfect, but because they all reinforced each other.

The defining question shifted from "How do we survive this?" to "How do we use this disruption to dominate our market?"

That's what integration creates.

Five Transformations When Integration Works

Integration isn't just about having all five ingredients present. It's about how they amplify each other. Here's what changes when organizations move from fragmented capabilities to integrated systems:

1. From Sequential to Simultaneous

Without integration: First we innovate (IDEAS), then we execute (SPEED), then we train people (TALENT), then we market it (DISTINCTION), then we lead the change (LEADERSHIP). Sequential. Slow. Vulnerable to disruption at every handoff.

With integration: All five happen simultaneously. Innovation teams include the people who will execute. Speed creates the urgency that drives talent development. Distinction emerges from the work itself, not marketing spin. Leadership isn't waiting at the end—it's embedded throughout.

2. From Addition to Multiplication

When ingredients operate independently, their impact adds up: 20 + 20 + 20 + 20 + 20 = 100. That's respectable. It might even be enough to survive.

But when they integrate, the math changes: 20 × 20 × 20 × 20 × 20 = 3,200,000. That's not hyperbole. That's what happens when innovation drives speed, speed develops talent, talent creates distinction, and leadership amplifies everything.

The difference between addition and multiplication is the difference between incremental improvement and exponential advantage.

3. From Fragile to Antifragile

Organizations with isolated capabilities are fragile. Take away their innovation team, and IDEAS die. Lose a few key leaders, and LEADERSHIP evaporates. A single weak ingredient can collapse the entire system.

Organizations with integrated capabilities become antifragile. They don't just survive disruption, they get stronger from it. When market conditions change, their SPEED allows rapid adjustment. When competitors attack, their TALENT adapts faster. When technology shifts, their IDEAS and DISTINCTION evolve together.

Stress reveals fragility. Stress creates strength when systems are integrated.

4. From Episodic to Continuous

Most organizations treat improvement as episodic: quarterly innovation sprints, annual talent reviews, periodic leadership development, scheduled strategy sessions. They turn capabilities on and off like light switches.

Integrated organizations make improvement continuous. Every project develops talent. Every challenge demands innovation. Every interaction reinforces distinction. Every day builds leadership capability. The five ingredients become how work happens, not something separate from work.

5. From Compliance to Commitment

When each ingredient is managed separately, innovation by one team, speed by another, talent by HR, distinction by marketing, leadership by executives, people comply with initiatives. They do what's required. They check boxes.

When ingredients integrate into how people actually work, compliance transforms into commitment. People don't execute someone else's innovation; they contribute their own IDEAS. They don't wait for permission to move fast, they take ownership of SPEED. They don't attend mandatory training, they actively develop TALENT because it makes them more valuable.

The shift from compliance to commitment is the shift from managing people to unleashing them.

How to Spot Integration Gaps (Before They Kill You)

Most organizations don't fail because they lack capabilities. They fail because their capabilities don't work together. Here are five patterns that predict failure:

Pattern 1: Externalized Change

Listen to how people talk: "They need to innovate more." "They should move faster." "They aren't developing talent." When change is something other people need to do, integration is impossible.

The tell: People score themselves 30-40% higher on the Kryptonite Scorecard than others score them. Everyone thinks they're accountable. Nobody thinks the team is.

Pattern 2: Meeting Theater

Lots of meetings. Lots of planning. Lots of discussion. Very little action. When talk replaces execution, integration fails.

The tell: Ask anyone what decisions came out of this week's meetings. If they struggle to name three clear actions with owners and deadlines, you're watching performance art, not executing strategy.

Pattern 3: False Urgency

Everything is urgent. Every project is critical. Every initiative is top priority. When everything is urgent, nothing is urgent. True urgency is focused, intentional, and aligned. False urgency creates chaos that masquerades as speed.

The tell: People are exhausted but results aren't improving. Lots of motion. Minimal momentum.

Pattern 4: The Leadership Bottleneck

Every decision waits for senior approval. Every innovation requires executive buy-in. Every risk needs permission from above. When leadership concentrates at the top, integration can't scale.

The tell: Smart, capable people waiting. Waiting for clarity. Waiting for approval. Waiting for direction. Meanwhile, competitors who distributed leadership are already moving.

Pattern 5: Self-Score Inflation

Ask individuals how they're doing on IDEAS, SPEED, TALENT, DISTINCTION, and LEADERSHIP. Most give themselves A's and B's. Ask about the team. Suddenly it's C's and D's. This gap, between how we see ourselves and how we see the collective, is the integration killer.

The tell: "I'm accountable, but they're not." If everyone believes this, integration is a fantasy.

Three Patterns That Predict Success

Just as failure leaves fingerprints, so does success. Organizations that achieve true integration share three patterns:

Success Pattern 1: Executive Alignment Before Rollout

The fatal mistake: Senior leaders cascade a message they don't personally believe or can't articulate. The organization sees through it instantly.

Successful organizations don't announce integration initiatives until executives can explain why all five ingredients matter, how they connect, and what they're personally doing differently. Not talking points. Conviction.

Success Pattern 2: Radical Candor About Current State

Organizations that successfully integrate don't sugarcoat the Kryptonite Scorecard results. They share the brutal facts: "Our Innovation Score is 12 out of 60. Our Integration Score is 8 out of 50. We're vulnerable, and here's the evidence."

This honesty creates the urgency that drives real change. Sugarcoating creates complacency that enables extinction.

Success Pattern 3: Disciplined Deployment

Organizations that achieve integration don't launch with a big event and hope for the best. They deploy systematically: pilot teams, measure results, adjust based on feedback, scale what works, kill what doesn't.

They treat deployment like product development: prototype, test, iterate, improve, scale. Not like a motivational speech: announce, inspire, move on.

The Kryptonite Scorecard: Measuring What Integration Looks Like

You can't improve what you don't measure. The Kryptonite Scorecard (Appendix A) gives you a practical tool to assess where you stand on all five ingredients and calculate your Integration Score.

Here's why the Integration Score matters more than your individual ingredient scores:

An organization with 40 on IDEAS, 40 on SPEED, 40 on TALENT, 40 on DISTINCTION, and 10 on LEADERSHIP gets an Integration Score of 10. One weak ingredient limits everything.

An organization with 30 on every ingredient gets an Integration Score of 30. Balanced strength beats isolated excellence.

The Scorecard forces the honest conversation most organizations avoid: Are we truly integrated, or are we just collecting capabilities?

Use it. Score yourself. Score your team. Compare the results. The gap between self-perception and reality is where the work begins.

· · ·

COMING UP IN CHAPTER 9:

In the next chapter, we shift from understanding the Kryptonite defense to deploying it in the real world. You'll get a practical, week-by-week roadmap for implementing everything you've learned. Not theory. Not inspiration. Actual deployment.

Let's build your 90-day future-proofing plan.

DEPLOYMENT

Your 90-Day Future-Proofing Plan

THE NOTEBOOK IN THE DRAWER

Jennifer and her colleague David invited me to lunch three weeks after their team attended my three-day workshop.

We met at a restaurant near their office. Jennifer, a regional marketing director for a mid-sized financial services company, brought her notebook, the same one she'd filled with ideas during the workshop.

Over three days, her team had worked through the 7-Sided Pincer Movement, assessed their vulnerabilities, mapped their Kryptonite defense, and scored themselves on integration. Her integration score was 38 out of 50. Not bad. Room for improvement, but she had the foundation.

She opened the notebook on the table between us.

"This is exactly what we need," she said. "I can see how all five ingredients work together now. I know what we need to do."

"That's great," I said. "So what's your first action when you get back to the office this afternoon?"

She paused. Flipped through pages.

David jumped in. "Well, we need to talk to the rest of the team about what we learned. And Jennifer should probably brief her boss. And then we need to figure out priorities because we can't do everything at once. Maybe form a task force? Or should we start with one ingredient and build from there? Actually, we should probably create a presentation for the executive team first…"

I stopped them.

"That's how good ideas die. You're about to turn execution into a planning project."

They both looked up, surprised.

"What you need isn't another planning session. You need a deployment plan. Week one, day one, hour one. What are you actually going to DO?"

Six months later, Jennifer called me.

"Mike, I never deployed anything. We got back to the office, got pulled into three urgent projects, and the notebook ended up in a drawer. I had everything I needed. I just never executed."

This chapter exists so you don't become Jennifer.

WHY I'M QUALIFIED TO WRITE THIS CHAPTER

Before I tell you how to deploy, you should know why I have such a strong bias toward execution.

I was the Regional Practice Leader for the Execution Practice at FranklinCovey, where we walked alongside clients helping them implement the Four Disciplines of Execution. Not consult. Not advise. Walk alongside them through actual implementation.

I've seen brilliant strategies die in PowerPoint. I've watched executives nod enthusiastically in workshops, then do absolutely nothing when they return to their offices. I've facilitated three-day offsites that produced zero behavior change.

I've also seen organizations that looked less prepared, with fewer resources and smaller teams, execute relentlessly and dominate their markets.

The difference was never strategy. It was always deployment.

I have spent 27 years watching that gap swallow careers. Not 27 months. Twenty-seven years, across 34 Fortune 50 companies, working alongside Dr. John Kotter, Dr. Stephen Covey, Jim Kouzes and Tom Peters, the people who built the frameworks this book is built on. The single most consistent finding across all of it: the professionals and organizations that survive disruption are not the ones with the best ideas. They are the ones who deploy.

So when I say you need a deployment system, I'm not giving you theory. I'm giving you what actually works when the workshop ends and real life begins.

Because otherwise, we're just wasting our time.

THE DEPLOYMENT TRAP

Here's the uncomfortable truth about transformation. Most people fail not because they lack knowledge, but because they lack a deployment system.

You now understand the 7-Sided Pincer Movement. You know the 5-Ingredient Kryptonite defense. You've assessed your integration. You have more knowledge than 95% of professionals about how to future-proof your career.

And if you close this book right now and go back to your normal routine, absolutely nothing will change.

Because knowing what to do and actually doing it are separated by the hardest gap in business: execution.

That gap is not a luxury problem anymore. In the week I completed this manuscript, 39 companies announced layoffs totaling more than 600,000 jobs. The CEO of Anthropic warned that AI could spike unemployment 10 to 20 percent within five years, naming lawyers, consultants, and finance professionals specifically. Jack Dorsey cut half of Block's workforce and called it a blueprint for the industry. These are not distant warnings. They are current events. The professionals who survive this wave will not be the ones who understood it was coming. They will be the ones who deployed a response before it arrived.

This chapter gives you the deployment system. Not inspiration. Not theory. A week-by-week, action-by-action roadmap that takes you from "I understand this" to "I'm living this."

WHAT REAL DEPLOYMENT LOOKS LIKE

Let me show you what deployment actually looks like when it works — and when it doesn't. Not theory. Real moments from 27 years of watching organizations try to change.

The Team That Deployed in 48 Hours

I delivered a full-day workshop to a regional leadership team at a mid-sized manufacturing company. Twelve leaders, one day, the full Kryptonite framework. By the end of the afternoon, they

had assessed themselves, identified their weakest ingredient —
SPEED — and mapped three specific bottlenecks slowing every
major initiative.

The VP of Operations was a quiet woman named Sandra. She
had said almost nothing for most of the day. But in the final hour,
she raised her hand.

"I know exactly what I'm going to do Monday morning," she said.
"We have a standing Tuesday approval meeting that takes two
weeks out of every decision cycle. I'm canceling it and replacing
it with a 24-hour email decision protocol. Anyone can escalate
in 24 hours. Otherwise we move."

I asked her if she needed organizational permission.

"It's my meeting," she said. "I called it. I can cancel it."

Two weeks later, her team had cut their average decision cycle
from 18 days to 4. Three months later, they had launched two
initiatives that had been sitting in planning for over a year.

Sandra didn't wait for perfect conditions. She didn't ask for a task
force to study the problem. She identified one bottleneck, eliminated it, and measured what happened. That's deployment.

The Executive Who Knew Everything and Did Nothing

I worked with a senior vice president at a large financial services
firm — I'll call him Robert — who attended three separate leadership programs over two years. He took meticulous notes. He
asked brilliant questions. He sent thoughtful follow-up emails.

His team hated working for him.

Not because he was cruel. Because he was perpetually preparing
to act. Every initiative needed one more study. Every decision
needed one more data point. Every change needed one more
alignment conversation before moving forward.

When I finally sat down with him directly, I asked a simple question: "What is the last decision you made in under 24 hours that moved something forward?"

He couldn't answer it.

Robert had confused learning with doing. He had mistaken preparation for action. He was, in the language of this book, highly skilled at acquiring knowledge about change and completely undeveloped in the discipline of executing it.

His Integration Score, had he taken the Kryptonite Scorecard honestly, would have shown strong IDEAS and moderate TALENT — with SPEED, DISTINCTION, and LEADERSHIP AT ALL LEVELS all in the developing or weak range.

He retired two years later. His team thrived under his successor within six months.

The lesson is not that Robert was a bad leader. The lesson is that knowledge without deployment is not leadership. It is an elaborate form of avoidance.

. . .

YOUR 90-DAY FUTURE-PROOFING PLAN

Ninety days is long enough to create real change, short enough to maintain urgency, and specific enough to hold yourself accountable.

This isn't everything you'll ever do. This is what you'll do in the next 90 days to shift from vulnerable to defensible.

WEEKS 1–2: Establish Your Baseline

Week 1, Day 1

Complete your Personal Kryptonite Scorecard from Chapter 8
Be brutally honest. This is for you, not for show.
Your INTEGRATION score is the most important number

Week 1, Days 2–5

Identify your lowest-scoring Kryptonite ingredient
Write down three specific examples of how this weakness has
    cost you in the past year
Identify one person who excels in this area — schedule 30 min-
    utes with them

Week 2

Map your current initiatives against the five ingredients
Identify disconnects — where initiatives don't support each other
Choose ONE integration to fix first: the one that will create the
    most immediate value

OUTCOME after Week 2: You know exactly where you stand, what's broken, and what to fix first.

WHAT WEEK ONE ACTUALLY FEELS LIKE

I want to be honest with you about something most deployment guides don't say.

Week one is uncomfortable.

You will sit down with the Kryptonite Scorecard and encounter the gap between who you believe yourself to be and what you actually do consistently. That gap is real. It is useful. And it will tempt you to either inflate your scores to close it artificially — or to feel so discouraged by it that you never start.

Don't do either.

The gap is not a verdict. It is a map. It tells you exactly where to start.

I have delivered this assessment to thousands of professionals across 27 years. The most common reaction in week one is not discouragement. It is relief. Relief that the problem is named. Relief that there is a clear starting point. Relief that the vague feeling of being behind or vulnerable or not quite prepared has been converted into something specific and actionable.

Name the gap. Own it. Then close it — one behavior at a time.

The One-Behavior Rule

The most common deployment mistake I see is trying to improve everything at once. A leader takes the Kryptonite Scorecard, identifies five weak behaviors, and launches five parallel improvement initiatives. By week three, all five have stalled.

The one-behavior rule is simple: identify your single lowest-scored behavior. Not your lowest ingredient — your lowest individual behavior within your lowest ingredient. That behavior becomes your entire focus for weeks one and two.

One behavior. Every day. For two weeks.

It sounds modest. It is not. Changing one ingrained behavior consistently over 14 days is harder than most people expect. The brain resists pattern disruption. Your calendar will conspire against you. Urgent things will compete for the time you allocated to important things.

If you can change one behavior consistently in two weeks, you have proven something to yourself: that you can actually do this. That proof is worth more than any framework or any keynote. It is the foundation everything else gets built on.

. . .

WEEKS 3–4: Quick Wins

Don't start with the hardest changes. Start with wins that build momentum.

Week 3

Implement ONE speed improvement — eliminate one approval step, one meeting, one bottleneck
Launch ONE idea you've been sitting on — prototype it in one day, test it within the week
Have ONE conversation you've been avoiding — feedback, conflict, uncomfortable truth

Week 4

Document your three wins from Week 3
Share them with your team or boss — claim credit, build reputation

Identify the next three quick wins and schedule them

OUTCOME after Week 4: Visible progress. Proof that this works. Momentum.

WEEKS 5–8: Build Your Integration

Now you tackle the integration you identified in Week 2.

Weeks 5–6: Connect Two Ingredients

Pick the two ingredients that aren't currently connected
Design one initiative that leverages both simultaneously
Example: Connect IDEAS + SPEED by implementing a "48-hour
   decision rule" for innovations under $5K
Example: Connect TALENT + DISTINCTION by training your
   team on the exact skills that deliver your unique value

Weeks 7–8: Test and Adjust

Launch your integration initiative
Measure results weekly
Adjust based on what's working and what's not
Document lessons learned

OUTCOME after Week 8: You've created one working integration. You have proof that the system works.

WEEKS 9–12: Scale and Embed

Weeks 9–10: Add a Third Ingredient

Look for opportunities to connect a third ingredient to your
   working integration

Example: Your IDEAS + SPEED integration now includes LEADER-
SHIP — you're teaching others how to make fast decisions
Train one other person on your integration approach

Weeks 11–12: Make It Standard Operating Procedure

Document your integration as a repeatable process
Share results with your team or organization
Build it into how you operate going forward
Schedule your next 90-day cycle

**OUTCOME after Week 12: Integration is now how you work — not
something you're trying to do.**

THE ACCOUNTABILITY SYSTEM

Plans without accountability are wishes. Here's how you ensure
you actually execute:

1. WEEKLY CHECK-INS

Every Monday morning, 15 minutes. Three questions only:

What did I commit to last week?
What did I actually do?
What's my commitment for this week?

2. FIND AN ACCOUNTABILITY PARTNER

Not your boss. Not your spouse. Someone who will ask hard
questions:

A colleague pursuing similar changes
A mentor who's been through transformation
A peer who won't let you off the hook

Meet or talk every two weeks. Share commitments. Report results. No exceptions.

3. VISIBLE TRACKING

Keep your Kryptonite Scorecard somewhere you see it daily
Update it monthly
Celebrate when scores improve
Investigate when they don't

. . .

THE ACCOUNTABILITY CONVERSATION MOST LEADERS AVOID

The accountability system in this chapter — weekly check-ins, an accountability partner, visible tracking — works. I have seen it work in organizations of every size and culture.

But there is a conversation that makes it work significantly better, and most leaders never have it.

It is the conversation where you tell someone who will not let you off the hook exactly what you are committing to and exactly what you are afraid of.

Not just the goals. The fears.

"I am committing to eliminating one approval bottleneck this week. And I am afraid that my boss will see it as me overstepping and that my team will take advantage of the faster process to push through decisions I should be reviewing."

That level of specificity — commitment plus fear — is what separates accountability conversations that produce change from accountability conversations that produce reassurance.

When you name the fear, two things happen. First, your accountability partner can help you think through whether the fear is realistic or distorted. Second, and more importantly, you have made the avoidance visible. You can no longer use the fear as an unconscious reason not to act, because you have named it out loud.

I learned this from Dr. Kotter, who understood that urgency requires honesty about what is actually in the way — not just what the plan says should happen, but what human psychology and organizational inertia will do to that plan the moment real life resumes.

Name the commitment. Name the fear. Then act anyway.

That is deployment.

. . .

OVERCOMING THE THREE BIGGEST OBSTACLES

OBSTACLE 1: "I DON'T HAVE TIME FOR THIS."

Reality check: You don't have time NOT to do this. The 7-Sided Pincer Movement is coming whether you prepare or not. The question is whether you'll be ready.

Solution: This plan requires 2–4 hours per week. Find them by eliminating one meeting, one report, or one activity that doesn't move you forward.

OBSTACLE 2: "MY ORGANIZATION WON'T SUPPORT THIS."

Reality check: You don't need organizational permission to develop IDEAS, increase your SPEED, build TALENT, create DISTINCTION, or demonstrate LEADERSHIP. These are personal capabilities that happen to benefit your organization.

Solution: Start with what you control. Prove it works. Others will notice.

OBSTACLE 3: "WHAT IF I FAIL?"

Reality check: You're already failing if you're standing still while disruption accelerates. The only real failure is not trying.

Solution: Reframe failure as learning. Every attempt teaches you something. Adjust and try again.

YOUR FIRST WEEK STARTS NOW

Jennifer eventually deployed her plan. It took a job change, a new boss who demanded action, and another six months of frustration before she finally started.

She told me later: "I wasted a year knowing what to do but not doing it. Don't let that happen to anyone else."

I think about the people I have worked with across 27 years who made it and those who didn't. The differentiator was almost never intelligence, resources, or timing. It was the willingness to act before they were certain, to deploy before they were ready, to move when everything in them said wait. The professionals who are reading this book in April 2026, when 600,000 jobs just evaporated in a single week, do not have the luxury of waiting until conditions are perfect. The conditions are never perfect. The deployment window is now.

So here's your first action:

Close this book. Open your calendar. Block 30 minutes tomorrow morning. Label it "Week 1, Day 1: Kryptonite Scorecard."

Then actually show up and do it.

Because the difference between people who survive disruption and people who get displaced isn't knowledge. It's deployment.

Your 90 days start now.

Those prepared need not fear the forces at work.

. . .

WHEN ORGANIZATIONS DEPLOY VS. WHEN THEY ANNOUNCE

There is a critical difference between deploying the Kryptonite framework and announcing it.

Announcing looks like this: a senior leader attends a keynote, returns energized, schedules an all-hands meeting, presents the framework to the team, declares it the new operating model, and assigns someone to own it.

Deploying looks like this: a senior leader attends a keynote, returns energized, identifies one specific behavior they personally are going to change in the next two weeks, changes it visibly, talks openly about what they're working on and why, and invites their team to do the same.

The difference is not scale. It is authenticity.

Organizations change when leaders model the change personally before asking anyone else to make it. Not in a speech. Not in a deck. In actual behavior, visible to the people watching.

I worked with a Chief Operating Officer — I'll call him Marcus — who understood this instinctively. After attending one of my workshops, he did something that surprised his entire organization. He sent an email to his direct reports with the subject line: 'My Kryptonite Score.'

In the email, he shared his actual scores. IDEAS: 41. SPEED: 28. TALENT: 44. DISTINCTION: 35. LEADERSHIP: 47. Integration Score: 19.

He wrote: 'My SPEED score is embarrassing. I have been the bottleneck on at least a dozen decisions in the past quarter. I am committing to one change starting Monday: any decision under $50,000 that has sat with me for more than 48 hours gets made by my direct report without my approval. I will report back in 30 days on how it went.'

His team was stunned. Not by the scores — by the honesty.

Within two weeks, three of his direct reports had voluntarily shared their own scores. Within 60 days, the team had identified and eliminated six recurring bottlenecks. The deployment didn't start with a program. It started with a leader telling the truth about himself.

That is the kind of urgency that activates the Maybes. Not a mandate. Not a program. A leader being visibly, specifically, honestly committed to their own growth.

. . .

THE 20/60/20 REALITY

Every organization deploys along a bell curve. Understanding this pattern is essential to deployment success.

The top 20% are your Models. They embrace change immediately. They experiment with IDEAS, move with SPEED, develop TALENT, create DISTINCTION, and demonstrate LEADERSHIP without being asked. They're already doing much of what the Kryptonite framework describes.

The middle 60% are your Maybes. They're watching. They want to see if leadership is serious. They want to know if this will actually work. They need proof before they commit.

The bottom 20% are your Nevers. They won't engage no matter what. Some are actively resistant. Some are just checked out. Either way, they're not moving.

Here's the deployment mistake that kills most initiatives. Leaders rely exclusively on the Models to drive change. The Models jump in enthusiastically. They take on extra work. They champion the framework. They try to pull everyone else along.

Then they burn out. Because the Maybes are still watching. The Nevers aren't helping. And the Models are doing everyone's work.

When your Models disengage, your initiative dies. Not because the framework doesn't work. Because you asked 20% of the organization to carry 100% of the change.

Successful deployment activates the Maybes. That's where victory lives.

The Fatal Mistake: Skipping Urgency

I learned this from Dr. John Kotter decades ago, and it's proven true in every transformation I've seen. You must create urgency before you roll out strategies.

Most organizations do it backward. They develop the perfect deployment plan. They create the comprehensive roadmap. They design the training. Then they launch it to an organization that doesn't understand why any of this matters.

Without urgency, the 90-Day Plan becomes a suggestion. The Kryptonite Scorecard becomes optional. The five ingredients become another flavor of the month.

True urgency isn't panic. It's the focused understanding that this matters now. That standing still is riskier than moving forward. That distinct or extinct isn't a tagline—it's reality.

Create that urgency first. Everything else follows.

Three Obstacles That Kill Deployment in the First Month

Most deployment failures happen fast. Here's what derails even well-designed initiatives within 30 days:

Obstacle 1: The Crisis That Wasn't Planned

Week two of deployment, a major client threatens to leave. Or a key executive quits. Or a product fails. The crisis demands immediate attention. The deployment gets shelved.

The organization learns: Leadership doesn't really believe this matters. When things get hard, we abandon it. The Maybes stop watching. The Nevers feel validated.

Obstacle 2: The Market Shift

Competitors launch something new. Customer preferences change. Technology disrupts the model. Suddenly everyone's focused on the external threat, and internal development feels like a luxury.

Irony: This is exactly when you need integrated IDEAS, SPEED, TALENT, DISTINCTION, and LEADERSHIP most. But if deployment isn't embedded yet, market shifts kill it.

Obstacle 3: The Leadership Change

The executive who championed the framework leaves. Or gets promoted. Or shifts focus to another priority. The new leader wants to make their own mark. The Kryptonite deployment becomes "the old regime's thing."

Dead in 60 days.

The Real Obstacle: Leaders Not Equipped
for Voluntary Behavior Change

The obstacles above are real. But they're symptoms. The actual problem runs deeper.

Most leaders are experts at managing compliance. Hit this number. Follow this process. Complete this project. They know how to cascade goals, measure KPIs, and hold people accountable to metrics.

But deploying the Kryptonite framework isn't about compliance. It's about voluntary behavior change. You can't mandate that someone demonstrates LEADERSHIP AT ALL LEVELS. You can't force people to innovate (IDEAS) or create DISTINCTION. You can't compel judgment, empathy, or strategic thinking (TALENT).

This requires a different kind of leadership. One that creates the conditions where people choose to change. Where they want to develop. Where they see the personal benefit in becoming distinct.

Most leaders haven't been trained for this. They know how to drive execution. They don't know how to inspire evolution.

That's not a criticism. It's reality. And it's fixable.

How to Activate the Maybes: Three Questions
They Need Answered

The middle 60%, the Maybes, will move when three questions get answered convincingly:

Question 1: Is leadership really serious about this?

They've seen initiatives come and go. They've watched leaders announce priorities that disappeared within months. They need proof this is different.

Answer it with: Consistent executive behavior. Visible resource allocation. Real consequences when the framework gets ignored.

Time investment from senior leaders. Public commitment that doesn't waver when obstacles emerge.

Question 2: Will this actually work?

They need evidence. Not case studies from other companies. Proof from inside their own organization that deploying the Kryptonite framework produces results.

Answer it with: Quick wins from pilot teams. Visible improvements in Integration Scores. Measurable changes in speed, innovation, or market response. Stories from peers they respect about how the framework helped solve real problems.

Question 3: What happens if I fail?

This is the unspoken question. If I try to innovate and it doesn't work, will I be punished? If I move fast and make a mistake, will my career suffer? If I take ownership beyond my authority and it backfires, what then?

Answer it with: Psychological safety. Public celebration of smart failures. Leaders who model vulnerability by sharing their own learning edges. Systems that reward experimentation, not just success.

It Is Hard Work

Everything in this chapter points to a truth most leadership books won't say directly. Deploying the Kryptonite framework is hard work.

Not complicated. Hard. There's a difference.

It's hard because you're asking people to change how they think, how they work, and how they see themselves. That's not a 90-day project. It's not a training program you check off. It's ongoing development that requires sustained attention, honest feedback, and the courage to look at brutal facts.

It's hard because obstacles will emerge. Crises will compete for attention. Markets will shift. Leaders will change. And you'll have to keep going anyway.

It's hard because the Maybes won't move until they see proof, the Models will burn out if you rely on them exclusively, and the Nevers will actively resist or passively disengage no matter what you do.

But here's what makes it worth it. The alternative is extinction.

Organizations that don't develop IDEAS get commoditized. Organizations that lack SPEED get outmaneuvered. Organizations that don't develop TALENT get automated. Organizations without DISTINCTION get replaced. Organizations that concentrate LEADERSHIP at the top get outpaced by those who distribute it throughout.

The work is hard. But those prepared need not fear the forces at work.

And that preparation starts with deployment.

. . .

COMING UP: THE FINAL CHAPTER

In the final chapter, we return to where we started: the Ghost Port of Yangshan, Mikey Calabrese, Chen Wei, and the choice that defines everything.

Distinct or Extinct. Which will you choose?

THE CHOICE

Distinct or Extinct

"It is not the strongest of the species that survives, nor the most intelligent. It is the one most adaptable to change."

— CHARLES DARWIN

PHILADELPHIA, PENNSYLVANIA — PRESENT DAY

The old row house in South Philly looks almost exactly as it did in 1956. Same brick facade. Same narrow front steps. Same neighborhood where generations of longshoremen raised their families.

But if you look closely, things have changed.

The house is owned by Mikey Calabrese Jr., now 77 years old. He never worked the docks like his father. By the time he was old enough, containerization had already begun its systematic dismantling of the longshoreman profession.

Mikey Sr. saw it coming, eventually. Not soon enough to save his own career, but soon enough to change his son's trajectory.

"My father sat me down when I was sixteen," Mikey Jr. told me when I interviewed him for this book. "He said, 'The docks are dying, son. Don't follow me there. Learn something the machines can't do.'"

So Mikey Jr. became a plumber. Then learned HVAC repair. Then started his own business. Eventually employed twelve people. Sold the business three years ago for enough money to retire comfortably.

"My father gave me the greatest gift," he said. "He told me the truth before it was too late."

Mikey Sr. died in 1989. He never fully recovered from losing his identity as a longshoreman. But he made sure his son didn't inherit his fate.

That's one kind of legacy.

SHANGHAI, CHINA — PRESENT DAY

Chen Wei no longer works at Yangshan Port.

The AI upgrade rolled out six months after we left him in Chapter 1. As predicted, the control room that once required five supervisors now requires two. Chen wasn't one of them.

But Chen's story doesn't end there.

Unlike the crane operators who simply disappeared when automation arrived, Chen saw the pattern. He had watched his grandfather's stories become obsolete. He had watched the crane operators vanish. He recognized he was next.

So he made a choice.

While still employed at Yangshan, Chen started learning AI systems architecture. Not just how to monitor the systems, but how they were built, how they learned, how they failed, and most importantly, how to optimize them.

He took online courses at night. Earned certifications. Built relationships with the AI vendors who supplied Yangshan's systems.

When the layoff notice came, he already had three job offers.

Today, Chen works for the company that builds the AI systems that replaced him. He consults with ports worldwide, helping them implement automation while training the humans who remain to work alongside the machines rather than compete with them.

He makes three times what he made as a supervisor.

"I learned from history," he told me via video call. "My grandfather couldn't adapt because he didn't see change coming. The crane operators couldn't adapt because they resisted too long. I adapted because I saw the pattern and moved before I was forced to."

That's another kind of legacy.

THE PATTERN THAT REPEATS

Mikey Calabrese Sr. and Chen Wei faced the same fundamental threat, separated by 70 years and 7,000 miles. Technology changed the equation of value in their industries. The skills that made them valuable became obsolete. Their jobs, their identities, and their futures hung in the balance.

The only difference was timing and awareness.

Mikey didn't see it coming until too late. Chen saw it coming and acted.

Now it's your turn.

The 7-Sided Pincer Movement, AI accelerating all six other forces, is doing to knowledge work exactly what containerization did to longshoremen and what automation did to port supervisors. The equation of value is changing in your industry right now.

I have tracked these forces for 27 years. Not 27 months. In that time, I have watched disruption reshape industry after industry, inside Intel, Apple, PepsiCo, Caterpillar, and 30 other Fortune 50 companies, working alongside Dr. John Kotter, Dr. Stephen Covey, Jim Kouzes and Tom Peters. The pattern is always the same. The people who saw it coming and acted are the ones telling the story. The ones who waited are the cautionary tale.

I finished writing this book in a week when 39 companies announced more than 600,000 layoffs driven by AI. The CEO of Anthropic warned on national television that unemployment could spike 10 to 20 percent within five years. Jack Dorsey cut half his workforce and called it a blueprint. These are not harbingers of a future threat. They are dispatches from the present one.

Then Oracle announced cuts of 20,000 to 30,000 employees. Not because the company was in trouble — its contracted future revenue had grown 433 percent year over year. Oracle was making a deliberate trade: people for AI infrastructure. One internal pilot had replaced 47 database administrators with three senior architects supervising automated systems. When a 47-year-old institution that runs the data backbone of corporate America makes that trade by choice, we are no longer talking about disruption as a future event. We are talking about policy. The Pincer has arrived at the front door of the companies that run every other company.

The question isn't whether you'll be affected. The question is whether you'll be Mikey or Chen.

· · ·

THE DATA IS NO LONGER THEORETICAL

I want to be precise about what the evidence shows right now, because the numbers have arrived faster than most predictions anticipated.

In August 2025, the St. Louis Federal Reserve published a study that plotted every major occupation on two axes: how exposed the role is to AI capability, and how much unemployment in that category has risen since 2022. The correlation was 0.47. When researchers used actual AI adoption data rather than theoretical capability assessments, the correlation jumped to 0.57.

The more AI can do your job, the more your unemployment has already risen. That is not a prediction. That is a measured outcome from the Federal Reserve.

But here is the part of that study that matters most for this book: office and administrative workers had nearly the same AI exposure as computer and math workers. Their unemployment barely moved. Same technology. Different response. The tool is identical. The outcome is not.

That is the entire argument of this book, confirmed by the Federal Reserve with a correlation coefficient.

Eric Schmidt, the former CEO of Google, described the shape of what is coming in terms that every organization needs to understand. He said we are heading toward a small number of very large companies and a massive number of very small companies. The middle disappears. When AI can do the work, organizations simply do not need as many people. Teams that needed ten junior professionals now run with two seniors and an AI system. The compression is not coming. It is happening.

Stanford University research found a 20 percent drop in hiring for early-career professionals in AI-exposed roles since late 2022. Some organizations report that AI now writes 70 to 90 percent of their product code. The entry-level position — the role that once taught the next generation how to think — is quietly disappearing.

None of this is designed to frighten you. It is designed to be honest with you. The people who thrive in this environment are not the ones who were warned most loudly. They are the ones who took the warning seriously and acted.

• • •

TWO PATHS, ONE CHOICE

At the beginning of this book, I told you that disruption creates two paths:

The path of those who become distinct.
The path of those who become extinct.

Let me show you what each path actually looks like.

The Path to Extinct

You continue doing what you've always done, assuming your expertise protects you

You watch AI handle more of your tasks but tell yourself you're still needed

You resist learning new skills because you're already good at what you do

You blend into the sea of sameness, offering what everyone else offers

You wait for your organization to tell you what to do

You treat the five Kryptonite ingredients as interesting ideas but never deploy them

You stay busy but not valuable

You wake up one day to a reorganization, a layoff notice, or a market shift that eliminates your role

You realize too late that "expert in obsolete skills" is not a marketable position

This isn't speculation. This is happening right now to thousands of professionals who are watching their industries transform while they stand still.

The Path to Distinct

You see disruption coming and study it rather than deny it

You assess yourself honestly using the Kryptonite Scorecard

You develop IDEAS relentlessly, innovating before you're forced to

You operate with SPEED, making decisions and executing faster than your peers

You build TALENT continuously, especially capabilities AI can't replicate

You create DISTINCTION through The Big 3: dramatically different, overt benefit, proven value

You demonstrate LEADERSHIP regardless of title, taking ownership of outcomes

You integrate all five ingredients so they multiply rather than add

You deploy systematically using the 90-day framework

You become the person others come to when disruption hits because you've already adapted

This isn't theory. This is the pattern of every person and organization I've seen thrive through 27 years of transformation.

The Pattern Repeats

The choice between distinct and extinct plays out at every level. Businesses. Sports teams. Entire industries. Individuals. The pattern is consistent: Those who integrate all five ingredients survive and thrive. Those who don't, disappear.

Here's what that looks like in practice:

Business: Reinvention Beats Protection

Netflix started by mailing DVDs. When streaming technology emerged, they didn't protect their DVD business. They cannibalized it. They invested in IDEAS (original content), moved with SPEED (infrastructure build-out), developed TALENT (data science and content creation capabilities), created DISTINC-TION (binge-watching culture, algorithm-driven recommendations), and distributed LEADERSHIP (empowering teams to make billion-dollar content decisions).

Blockbuster protected their retail footprint. They saw the same technology. They had the same opportunity. They chose to defend what they had instead of building what customers wanted.

Netflix: $280 billion market cap. Blockbuster: Bankrupt.

Business: Redefine the Category

In 2007, BlackBerry dominated smartphones with 43% market share. They had DISTINCTION, the device presidents and CEOs used. They had a clear value proposition: secure business communication.

Then Apple launched the iPhone. They didn't compete on BlackBerry's terms (business email). They redefined what a phone could be: computer, camera, entertainment system, life organizer. They integrated IDEAS (touchscreen interface, app ecosystem), SPEED (annual hardware refresh, constant software updates), TALENT (developer community creating millions of apps), DISTINCTION (user experience, design, ecosystem lock-in), and LEADERSHIP (vision from Jobs that became distributed throughout the organization).

BlackBerry protected keyboards. Apple owned the future.

Business: Speed Beats Size

Sears was America's largest retailer. They had resources, real estate, brand recognition, customer relationships. Massive advantages.

Amazon started in a garage selling books. But they integrated all five ingredients: relentless IDEAS (Prime, AWS, Alexa, one-click ordering), obsessive SPEED (two-day shipping became one-day became same-day), systematic TALENT development (leadership principles, bar raisers, working backwards), clear DISTINCTION (customer obsession, vast selection, convenience), and distributed LEADERSHIP (two-pizza teams, ownership mentality).

Same pattern played out with Toys R Us and Borders. Size without integration is vulnerability disguised as strength.

Sports: Evolution Never Stops

Tom Brady won seven Super Bowls across 23 seasons. Not because he was the most physically talented quarterback. Because he constantly evolved. Every off-season, he reinvented some aspect of his game. Nutrition. Training. Film study. Mechanics. Mental approach. Leadership style.

He integrated IDEAS (trying new training methods, diet approaches), SPEED (quick release, rapid decision-making, fast adaptation to defensive schemes), TALENT (relentless skill development, studying film like a PhD dissertation), DISTINCTION (clutch performance, leadership presence), and LEADERSHIP (elevating everyone around him, making practice squad receivers look like All-Pros).

Dozens of more physically gifted quarterbacks washed out of the league. They relied on talent alone. Brady integrated everything.

Sports: Innovation Levels the Playing Field

The 2002 Oakland A's had one of baseball's smallest budgets. They couldn't compete on resources. So they revolutionized how baseball evaluated talent. Moneyball wasn't about statistics. It was about integrating IDEAS (sabermetrics, market inefficiencies), SPEED (rapid player evaluation and acquisition), TALENT (developing undervalued players), DISTINCTION (completely different approach to team building), and

LEADERSHIP (getting traditional baseball people to embrace radical change).

They won 103 games with a payroll that ranked 24th. Not once. Repeatedly. Then the rest of baseball copied them. Now everyone uses analytics. The A's distinction became commoditized—which proves the point. You must continuously evolve your integration to stay distinct.

Individual: Inventing the Future Then Killing It

Kodak engineer Steve Sasson invented the digital camera in 1975. Kodak owned the technology. They owned the patents. They owned the future.

Then they buried it. Digital threatened their film business. Film generated 70% of profits. So they protected what they had instead of building what was coming.

By 2012, Kodak filed for bankruptcy. The company that invented digital photography was destroyed by it.

Meanwhile, companies that integrated digital technology, Canon, Nikon, Sony, and eventually smartphone makers, captured the market Kodak abandoned.

Individual: Technology Adoption Separates Survivors

When Uber launched, taxi drivers faced a choice. Some saw it as a threat and resisted. They lobbied for regulations. They complained about unfair competition. They defended medallion values.

Other drivers saw it as a tool and adapted. They became Uber drivers. They used the platform to find customers, manage schedules, and maximize earnings. They integrated IDEAS (flexible work strategies), SPEED (rapid response to demand patterns), TALENT (customer service skills, route optimization),

DISTINCTION (high ratings, preferred driver status), and LEADERSHIP (taking ownership of their business within the platform).

The resisters lost their livelihoods. The adapters found new opportunities. Same disruption. Different responses. Different outcomes.

WHAT DISTINCT LOOKS LIKE AT THE INDIVIDUAL LEVEL

The case studies earlier in this chapter — Netflix, Apple, Amazon, Tom Brady, the Oakland A's — illustrate integration at scale. But the choice between distinct and extinct plays out just as clearly at the individual level, inside organizations most people have never heard of, in careers that never make the news.

Here are three professionals I have worked with directly. Their names have been changed. Their stories have not.

The HR Director Who Rewrote Her Role

When I met Patricia, she had been a Human Resources Director at a mid-sized healthcare system for eleven years. She was good at her job by every traditional measure — low turnover, strong compliance record, smooth onboarding processes. She was also, by her own honest assessment, completely replaceable.

"Everything I do," she told me during a workshop debrief, "could be done by a good HR software platform and two coordinators."

She was not wrong. And she knew it.

Over the following eighteen months, Patricia made a deliberate choice. She stopped optimizing her existing role and started building capabilities that her role had never required before. She studied workforce analytics deeply — not just HR metrics, but the connection between workforce composition, skill development, and organizational performance. She taught herself to read the organization's financial statements and connect people decisions to business outcomes. She built relationships with every department head to understand what capabilities their teams would need in three years, not just today.

When the organization went through a significant AI implementation eighteen months later, Patricia was the person the CEO called first. Not because she was the most senior. Because she was the only person who had mapped what the human side of that transition would require.

She was promoted to Chief People Officer. The role had not existed before. She built it by making herself distinct before anyone asked her to.

The Sales Manager Who Saw the Middle Disappearing

David had been a regional sales manager for a software company for eight years. He was consistently in the top quarter of performers. He had a strong team and a loyal book of business.

He also noticed something that made him uncomfortable. The company's AI tools were getting better at identifying prospects, generating outreach sequences, and predicting which accounts were most likely to close. Junior sales representatives were becoming less necessary. Senior representatives who could build complex enterprise relationships were becoming more valuable.

David was in the middle. Good enough to survive the first round of cuts. Not differentiated enough to be indispensable.

He made a decision. He spent the next year becoming the person at his company who understood, better than anyone else, how to sell to organizations going through AI transformation. He studied the subject relentlessly. He built a point of view about what those clients needed that went far beyond the software product he was selling. He started being asked to join executive conversations that had nothing to do with closing a deal and everything to do with helping a client think through a transformation challenge.

When his company restructured its sales organization eighteen months later, eliminating twelve of the twenty regional manager roles, David was not only retained — he was asked to lead the new enterprise transformation practice.

He had not waited to be saved. He had built something that made the question of saving him irrelevant.

The Engineer Who Trained His Replacement — and Survived

This story is harder. I share it because it is the most honest illustration of what the current environment actually requires.

Marcus was a senior software engineer at a large technology company. He was technically excellent, well-regarded, and had spent twelve years building deep expertise in a system that was central to the company's operations.

When his organization began an AI-driven efficiency initiative, Marcus was asked to participate in what the company called knowledge transfer sessions — structured interviews where experienced engineers documented their decision-making processes, their approaches to complex problems, their accumulated institutional knowledge.

Marcus participated fully. He was thorough and generous with what he shared. He believed he was helping the organization prepare for a transition that would eventually require his expertise to supervise and maintain.

Six months later, his team was eliminated. The knowledge he had transferred had been used to build AI workflows that could handle 80 percent of what his team had done. Three senior architects remained to manage the systems. The rest were let go.

Marcus was one of the three who stayed. Not by accident.

For the two years before the initiative began, Marcus had been doing something his colleagues had not. He had been building skills that existed above the level of the work he was documenting. Systems architecture. AI implementation oversight. The judgment to know when an automated system was making a decision that required human review and when it could be trusted to proceed independently.

His colleagues had optimized the work they were currently doing. Marcus had been building the capabilities required to supervise systems that would eventually do that work.

He did not know the restructuring was coming. He had simply asked himself, consistently, what skills would be valuable if the things he currently did became automated. Then he built those skills.

That is the Kryptonite Defense working in real time. Not as a reaction to disruption. As a preparation for it.

· · ·

YOUR TURN

Every example above illustrates the same truth. Integration of all five ingredients is what separates distinct from extinct.

Netflix integrated. Blockbuster didn't. Apple integrated. Black-Berry didn't. Amazon integrated. Sears didn't. Brady integrated.

Physically superior quarterbacks didn't. The A's integrated. Bigger-budget teams initially didn't. Uber drivers who thrived integrated. Those who fought the platform didn't.

Kodak invented the future and killed it. That's the cautionary tale. Having IDEAS isn't enough if you lack the courage to deploy them with SPEED, develop the TALENT to execute them, create the DISTINCTION they enable, and demonstrate the LEADERSHIP to overcome internal resistance.

Now it's your turn.

You have the framework. You have the Kryptonite Scorecard. You have the 90-Day Deployment Plan. You have examples of what integration looks like and what happens when it's missing.

The question isn't whether the seven-sided pincer is coming. It's here. AI isn't arriving. It's accelerating. The forces at work aren't theoretical. They're reshaping industries, redefining careers, and redistributing value right now.

The only question is: What will you do?

Will you integrate IDEAS, SPEED, TALENT, DISTINCTION, and LEADERSHIP AT ALL LEVELS? Or will you optimize one or two ingredients and hope it's enough?

Will you deploy systematically with urgency and discipline? Or will you announce the initiative and hope for the best?

Will you activate the Maybes and build momentum? Or will you burn out the Models and watch the initiative die?

Will you measure your Integration Score honestly and work to improve it? Or will you inflate your self-assessment and miss the gaps that will kill you?

The choice is yours. Distinct or extinct.

. . .

THE CHOICE YOU MAKE TODAY

Here's what makes this moment different from every other time you've read a business book or attended a workshop:

You can't pretend you don't know.

You understand the 7-Sided Pincer Movement. You know it's real, it's accelerating, and it's coming for your industry if it hasn't arrived already.

You have the 5-Ingredient Kryptonite defense. You know exactly what to do: IDEAS, SPEED, TALENT, DISTINCTION, LEADER-SHIP, integrated and deployed systematically.

You have the assessment tools to know where you stand today. You have the 90-day deployment plan to know what to do to-morrow.

You have everything Mikey Calabrese never had: warning, roadmap, and time to act.

So the choice is simple, though not easy:

Will you deploy, or will you delay?
Will you adapt, or will you hope?
Will you become distinct, or will you become extinct?

WHAT DISTINCT ACTUALLY LOOKS LIKE

IN SIX MONTHS

You've completed two 90-day cycles

Your Kryptonite integration score has improved by 20+ points

You've built a reputation as someone who executes, not just plans

You've developed at least one new capability that AI can't replicate

Your manager or clients notice you're different from your peers

IN ONE YEAR

You're known for something specific and valuable

People come to you for problems others can't solve

You're leading change initiatives regardless of your title

Your integration of all five ingredients is visible in your results

You're not worried about AI displacement because you've made yourself indispensable

IN THREE YEARS

You're doing work that didn't exist three years ago

You're creating opportunities rather than waiting for them

Your career trajectory is up and right while others' flatten

You're the person your organization can't afford to lose

You sleep well knowing you're prepared for whatever disruption comes next

This isn't motivational fantasy. This is what happens when you systematically build the five ingredients, integrate them, and deploy relentlessly.

WHAT EXTINCT ACTUALLY LOOKS LIKE

IN SIX MONTHS

You're still doing exactly what you're doing today
AI has quietly taken over three more tasks you used to do
Your company has announced another "efficiency initiative"
You notice your role feels less essential than it used to
You tell yourself you'll make changes "when things slow down"

IN ONE YEAR

Your department is "restructuring"
Competitors are doing what you do, faster and cheaper
You're attending workshops on change management while changing nothing
Your integration score is the same or worse
You're worried but still not acting

IN THREE YEARS

Your job has been automated, outsourced, or eliminated
You're competing for roles with people who adapted
Your resume looks impressive but obsolete
You're explaining in interviews why you didn't see this coming
You wish you had acted when you first read this book

*This isn't fear-mongering. This is the pattern I've watched repeat
for 27 years across every major disruption.*

THE CHOICE IS ALWAYS PERSONAL BEFORE IT IS PROFESSIONAL

Every case study in this chapter — from Netflix to Patricia to Marcus — illustrates the same fundamental truth.

The choice between distinct and extinct is never made at the organizational level first. It is made by an individual who decides, before anyone requires it, to build something that cannot be replaced.

Netflix did not become Netflix because of a corporate mandate to disrupt the DVD business. It became Netflix because Reed Hastings made a personal decision to build toward a future that did not yet exist rather than protect a present that was already working.

Patricia did not become a Chief People Officer because her organization decided to create the role. She became one because she made a personal decision to build the skills that would make that role necessary.

Marcus did not survive the restructuring because the company decided to protect him. He survived because he had made a personal decision, years earlier, to build above the level of his current work.

The organizations and professionals who become extinct almost always had the same opportunity. They simply made a different personal choice — to optimize what was working rather than build what was coming.

That choice is available to you right now.

Not the organizational version of it. The personal version. The one you make alone, before anyone is watching, before anyone requires it, before the disruption makes it urgent.

The people who survive disruption make that choice early. The people who don't make it late — or not at all.

. . .

THE LEGACY QUESTION

Mikey Calabrese Sr. never got to answer the question I'm about to ask you.

He didn't have the warning. He didn't have time to prepare. The disruption moved faster than he could adapt.

But he did leave a legacy. He warned his son. He told the truth. He made sure the next generation had a chance to choose differently.

Now you get to answer the question:

What will your legacy be?

Will you be the one who saw disruption coming and adapted, becoming an example others follow?

Or will you be the cautionary tale, the person who had knowledge but never deployed, who had time but wasted it, who had a roadmap but never left the parking lot?

Your children, your team, your organization, they're watching. Not what you say. What you do.

YOUR MOVE

You have read the book. Now close it.
Open your calendar.

Block 30 minutes tomorrow morning.
Label it "Week 1, Day 1: Kryptonite Scorecard."
Then show up and do it.
That's the first move in choosing distinction over extinction.
Everything else follows from that one decision to act instead of delay.
The 7-Sided Pincer Movement is real.
The 5-Ingredient Kryptonite defense works.
The 90-day deployment plan is tested.

You have everything you need. The only question left is:
Will you use it?

. . .

Mikey Calabrese couldn't choose. The tide of disruption swept over him before he knew it was coming.

Chen Wei chose to adapt. Today he thrives.

You can choose.

Those prepared need not fear the forces at work.

Choose distinct.

Your future depends on it.

WHAT I KNOW AFTER 27 YEARS

I started learning about disruption when I was seven years old.

Not in a classroom. Not from a book. From a front-row seat watching the people around me make choices, and living with the consequences of those choices. I was always watching. My family, my parents, my neighbors. Trying to understand, even as a child, why some people made it and others didn't.

My family was wealthy. Not comfortably well-off, genuinely wealthy. Multiple homes. Yachts. A plane. New cars every year for everyone. Travel whenever we wanted. My father had built a company, and that company appeared, on the surface, to be producing extraordinary results.

I was a kid, but something always nagged at me. Even then, I could not fully reconcile what I was seeing. The lifestyle felt disconnected from what the business could realistically produce. I didn't have the vocabulary for it. But the feeling was there, a quiet, persistent sense that something did not add up.

I was right.

When I was eighteen years old, my family lost everything. Not gradually. Not over a painful year of slow decline. Within days. My father had made catastrophic financial decisions, and the life we had known simply collapsed. The homes, the boats, the cars, the security, gone. My mother, my three brothers, my sister, and I went from having everything handed to us to having nothing at all.

What happened next told me everything I needed to know about the rest of my life.

. . .

My siblings struggled for years after that moment. Some of them are still struggling today.

One of my brothers was among the most naturally gifted people I have ever known. Brilliant mind. Magnetic personality. Creative in ways that could have taken him anywhere. And he went nowhere. Not because the world failed him. Because he could not translate potential into action. He could describe exactly what he was going to do with a clarity and confidence that made everyone believe him. Then he would do nothing. Today he is penniless and owns nothing. Decades of potential, entirely unfulfilled.

Another brother watched what happened to our father and, instead of learning from it, replicated a version of it. He became a stockbroker. Within a year of his first job, he was arrested and stripped of his license. He had chosen the performance of success over its substance, the appearance of a thing rather than its reality. The consequences were swift and permanent.

I watched all of this. I had been watching my whole life.

What separated me from them was not intelligence. It was not talent. We grew up in the same house, with the same advantages and the same sudden collapse. The difference was a habit I had developed before I even understood what I was doing. I watched people relentlessly, trying to understand why some succeeded and others didn't. When I saw something that worked, I moved toward it. When I saw something that didn't, I moved away.

The week we lost everything; I did not flinch. I went door to door selling vacuum cleaners to feed myself.

Not because I had a plan. Not because I was fearless. Because I had spent years watching people wait for conditions to improve before they acted, and watching what that cost them. I had decided, without fully articulating it, that I would not be one of them.

. . .

I started formally tracking disruption in 1991.

Not because I had a framework for it. Not because I saw a book deal on the horizon. Because I kept watching smart, hardworking, talented people get blindsided by forces they had not seen coming, and I could not stop thinking about why.

I was at FranklinCovey then, walking alongside organizations trying to implement what Dr. Stephen Covey had taught about effectiveness and principle-centered living. The work was meaningful. But I kept noticing something the frameworks did not fully address. Even the most effective people could be made irrelevant by forces entirely outside their control. Being highly effective at the wrong thing, in the wrong moment, for an industry pointed in the wrong direction, was still a path to extinction.

So I started paying attention differently.

I watched ERP systems quietly eliminate entire layers of middle management. I watched globalization hollow out industries that had felt permanent. I watched the internet rewrite the rules of distribution, communication, and competition in less than a decade. I watched outsourcing send work overseas that a generation of professionals had built their identities around. And through all of it, I noticed the same pattern. The people who saw it coming had a choice. The people who didn't were simply swept away.

My colleagues used to joke about the way I clung to the words of the people I worked alongside, Covey, Kotter, Peters, Kouzes, Posner. It was not admiration for its own sake. It was the same instinct I had developed as a child. Find the people who actually know, watch them closely, take everything they offer, and put it to use.

Covey taught me that effectiveness is rooted in principles, not tactics, that lasting change comes from the inside out.

Kotter showed me what urgency actually looks like. Not panic, not pressure, but a focused understanding that standing still is the most dangerous thing you can do when the world is moving.

Peters reminded me that excellence is not a destination. It is a daily practice, sometimes uncomfortable, always demanding.

Kouzes and Posner showed me that leadership is not a position. It is a choice, made again and again, by people at every level.

By the time I was working directly with Dr. Kotter at Kotter International, I had come to understand something I have never stopped believing:

The most dangerous threat to any person or organization is not the disruption itself. It is the complacency that prevents them from seeing it.

That belief is why this book exists.

AI is not a new chapter in the disruption story. It is the acceleration of every chapter that came before it. The 7-Sided Pincer Movement is not a metaphor I invented to frighten people. It is the pattern I have spent 27 years watching converge. And for the first time in my career, all seven forces are moving simultaneously, at a pace that leaves very little margin for delay.

. . .

WHAT I ALSO KNOW

The people who prepare do not just survive disruption. They lead through it. They become the person others turn to. They build careers and organizations that look completely different five years from now, in the best possible way.

Every major disruption I have witnessed in my career created as many extraordinary opportunities as it eliminated roles. The question was never whether opportunity existed. The question was always whether the person standing in front of it was ready to claim it.

I think about my brother, the brilliant one, the one who could have done anything, often. Not with bitterness. With something closer to gratitude, because watching him shaped me more profoundly than any mentor or book ever could. He taught me, by example, who I did not want to be. He taught me that knowing what to do and doing it are separated by the hardest gap in the world. The gap between intention and action.

He never closed that gap. I have spent 27 years helping others close it.

You now have what Mikey Calabrese Sr. never had, and what my brother never used: warning, roadmap, and time.

Use it.

. . .

My wife has been my partner through every page of this book, and through every year of the work that made it possible. My sons Zack and Nick, and my stepchildren Brady and Brooke, have watched their father spend a career studying forces that most people prefer not to think about. I hope what they take from that is not the urgency, but the underlying conviction:

Preparation is an act of optimism.

It says, I believe the future is worth getting ready for. I believe I have something to contribute to it. I believe the work of becoming distinct is worth doing.

The future belongs to the people who take it seriously enough to get ready.

That is what I want for you. Not just survival. Not just relevance. I want you to be the one telling the story, from the other side of the disruption, looking back at the moment you decided to get ready, grateful you did.

. . .

Those prepared need not fear the forces at work.

Mike Evans
Pittsburgh, Pennsylvania
April 2026

THE KRYPTONITE SCORECARD™

THE KRYPTONITE SCORECARD™

What This Assessment Measures

The Kryptonite Scorecard measures your capability across the five ingredients that make professionals irreplaceable in the age of AI:

- **IDEAS** — Innovation, Advancement & Creativity
- **SPEED** — Strategic Velocity Without Panic
- **TALENT** — Irreplaceable Human Capabilities
- **DISTINCTION** — Escaping Commoditization
- **LEADERSHIP AT ALL LEVELS** — Distributed Ownership

This assessment provides two critical measurements:
1. Your score on each ingredient (maximum 60 points each)
2. Your Integration Score (maximum 50 points)

Key Insight: Your Integration Score matters more than individual scores.

Before You Begin: The Honesty Test

Over 27 years, I have noticed people score themselves 30-40% higher than colleagues score them.

The accountability paradox: I ask "Are you accountable?" Nobody says no. Then I ask "Does your team need more accountability?" 98% say yes. When people grade themselves: mostly A and B grades. When they grade their team: mostly C and D grades.

This is human nature. We see our intentions. Others see our behaviors.

As you complete this assessment, resist the temptation to:

- Score based on what you INTEND to do
- Rate yourself against the worst performer
- Blame circumstances for gaps

Instead:

- Score what you ACTUALLY do, consistently
- Hold yourself to the standard you hold others to
- Own your contribution to every gap

Human beings are the only living creatures with the capacity and propensity for self-deception. Be honest with your self-assessment. That is how we grow.

Professionals who transform score themselves honestly.

How to Score

Rate each behavior on frequency (1-10):

1-2 = Almost Never | 3-4 = Rarely | 5-6 = Sometimes | 7-8 = Usually | 9-10 = Almost Always

INGREDIENT #1: IDEAS

Innovation, Advancement & Creativity

1. I actively search for innovative ways to improve what I do, even when things are working well.

   YOUR SCORE (1-10): _____

2. I challenge legacy processes and ask "Why do we do it this way?" rather than accepting the status quo.

   YOUR SCORE (1-10): _____

3. I experiment with new approaches and methods, even when there is risk of failure.

    YOUR SCORE (1-10): _____

4. I seek out ideas and best practices from outside my immediate field or industry.

    YOUR SCORE (1-10): _____

5. I prototype and test ideas quickly rather than waiting for perfect conditions.

    YOUR SCORE (1-10): _____

6. I learn from failures quickly and move on to new ideas rather than dwelling on setbacks.

    YOUR SCORE (1-10): _____

IDEAS TOTAL SCORE: _____ /60

INGREDIENT #2: SPEED

Strategic Velocity Without Panic

7. I make decisions quickly based on 70% certainty rather than waiting for perfect information.

    YOUR SCORE (1-10): _____

8. I eliminate unnecessary approval steps and bureaucracy from my workflows.

    YOUR SCORE (1-10): _____

9. I move from decision to action rapidly, with minimal delay between "we should" and "we did."

    YOUR SCORE (1-10): _____

10. I create urgency without creating panic — people move fast, focused, intentional, aligned with top priorities and deliberately, but do not feel chaotic.

    YOUR SCORE (1-10): _____

11. I iterate and improve quickly rather than trying to perfect things before launch.

    YOUR SCORE (1-10): _____

12. I identify and remove bottlenecks that slow down progress for myself and my team.

    YOUR SCORE (1-10): _____

SPEED TOTAL SCORE: _____ /60

INGREDIENT #3: TALENT

Irreplaceable Human Capabilities

13. I continuously develop capabilities that AI cannot replicate (judgment, creativity, relationships, adaptive thinking).

    YOUR SCORE (1-10): _____

14. I build deep relationships that create trust and collaboration beyond what technology can facilitate.

    YOUR SCORE (1-10): _____

15. I demonstrate strategic judgment and contextual decision-making that goes beyond data analysis.

    YOUR SCORE (1-10): _____

16. I cultivate empathy and emotional intelligence in my interactions with others.

    YOUR SCORE (1-10): _____

17. I develop adaptive thinking — the ability to apply knowledge in new, unexpected situations.

    YOUR SCORE (1-10): _____

18. I hold myself accountable for outcomes and take ownership regardless of formal authority. I do not waste time playing the blame-game. I learn from failures and successes and keep moving forward.

    YOUR SCORE (1-10): _____

TALENT TOTAL SCORE: _____ /60

INGREDIENT #4: DISTINCTION

Escaping Commoditization

19. I can clearly articulate what makes my work dramatically different from others in my field.

    YOUR SCORE (1-10): _____

20. I deliver overt benefits that are immediately visible and valuable to others.

    YOUR SCORE (1-10): _____

21. I have proven, demonstrable results that show the impact of my distinct capabilities.

    YOUR SCORE (1-10): _____

22. I avoid doing what everyone else does — I deliberately create differentiation.

    YOUR SCORE (1-10): _____

23. I build specialized expertise in areas that are valuable but not widely developed.

   YOUR SCORE (1-10): _____

24. I make it easy for others to see and articulate what makes me irreplaceable.

   YOUR SCORE (1-10): _____

DISTINCTION TOTAL SCORE: _____ /60

INGREDIENT #5: LEADERSHIP AT ALL LEVELS

Distributed Ownership

25. I take ownership of outcomes regardless of whether I have formal authority. I go above and beyond what is required to achieve what matters most.

   YOUR SCORE (1-10): _____

26. I act without waiting for permission when I see opportunities or problems.

   YOUR SCORE (1-10): _____

27. I hold myself and others accountable for commitments and results. I model accountability and develop it in others.

   YOUR SCORE (1-10): _____

28. I challenge processes and decisions constructively, even when it is uncomfortable.

   YOUR SCORE (1-10): _____

29. I model and develop exemplary leadership capabilities in others, not just in myself.

   YOUR SCORE (1-10): _____

30. I demonstrate the behaviors I expect from others — I model what I advocate.

YOUR SCORE (1-10): ____

LEADERSHIP TOTAL SCORE: ____ /60

YOUR KRYPTONITE SCORECARD SUMMARY

Transfer your scores here:

IDEAS (Behaviors 1-6): ____ /60
SPEED (Behaviors 7-12): ____ /60
TALENT (Behaviors 13-18): ____ /60
DISTINCTION (Behaviors 19-24): ____ /60
LEADERSHIP (Behaviors 25-30): ____ /60
TOTAL SCORE: ____ /300

CALCULATE YOUR INTEGRATION SCORE

Your Integration Score measures how well your five ingredients work together.

This is MORE important than your individual scores.

Integration Score Formula:

Step 1: Identify your LOWEST ingredient score from above.
Step 2: Count how many ingredients scored within 10 points of your lowest score.
Step 3: Use this formula:
Integration Score = (Lowest Score × Number of Balanced Ingredients) ÷ 6

EXAMPLE:

Your scores: IDEAS=45, SPEED=42, TALENT=48, DISTINCTION=40, LEADERSHIP=44

- Lowest score = 40 (DISTINCTION)
- Ingredients within 10 points of 40: All five (40-50 range)
- Integration Score = $(40 \times 5) \div 6 = 33$

YOUR CALCULATION:

Lowest ingredient score: ______
Number of ingredients within 10 points: ______

YOUR INTEGRATION SCORE: ____ / 50

INTERPRETING YOUR SCORES

Individual Ingredient Scores (Maximum 60 each)

50-60: EXCEPTIONAL — You consistently demonstrate this ingredient at a high level

40-49: STRONG — You regularly demonstrate this ingredient

30-39: DEVELOPING — You demonstrate this ingredient inconsistently

20-29: WEAK — You rarely demonstrate this ingredient

0-19: CRITICAL GAP — This ingredient is largely absent from your work

Integration Score (Maximum 50)

This is your most important score. It measures how well your capabilities work together.

40-50: DISTINCT

Full integration achieved. Your ingredients multiply each other. You operate as a market-shaping professional. You do not just survive disruption — you use it to dominate.

30-39: STRONG

Most ingredients work together effectively. You have visible integration creating competitive advantage. Continue strengthening weakest ingredients.

20-29: DEVELOPING

Some ingredients present but not fully integrated. Capabilities exist but do not multiply each other. Focus on connecting your strongest ingredients.

0-19: VULNERABLE

Little to no integration. Individual ingredients are weak and disconnected. High risk of displacement. Immediate action required — start with Chapter 9 deployment plan. Which Chapters Should You Review?

Based on your LOWEST ingredient score, here is where to focus:

If IDEAS scored lowest:

Review Chapter 3 (IDEAS in detail). Focus on challenging status quo, rapid prototyping, and learning from failures quickly.

If SPEED scored lowest:

Review Chapter 4 (SPEED in detail). Focus on eliminating bureaucracy, creating urgency without panic, and moving from decision to action rapidly.

If TALENT scored lowest:

Review Chapter 5 (TALENT in detail). Focus on developing irreplaceable human capabilities: judgment, creativity, relationships, and adaptive thinking.

If DISTINCTION scored lowest:

Review Chapter 6 (DISTINCTION in detail). Review the Big 4 Questions and Brand You framework. Focus on creating visible, dramatic differentiation.

If LEADERSHIP scored lowest:

Review Chapter 7 (LEADERSHIP AT ALL LEVELS in detail). Focus on the Results Model and taking ownership regardless of formal authority.

If INTEGRATION scored lowest:

Review Chapter 8 (Integration). This is critical — you have pieces but they are not working together. Focus on how the five ingredients multiply each other.

For ALL scores:

Review Chapter 9 for the 90-day deployment plan. This shows you how to systematically improve any ingredient or behavior.

WARNING SIGNS IN YOUR SCORES

WARNING SIGN #1: Wide Score Variation

If your highest and lowest ingredient scores differ by more than 20 points, you have an integration problem.

Example: IDEAS=55, SPEED=50, TALENT=48, DISTINCTION=52, LEADERSHIP=28

The Issue: Your capabilities do not work together. You are brilliant at innovation but terrible at distributed leadership. This creates bottlenecks and limits your impact.

WARNING SIGN #2: Low Integration Despite High Individual Scores

If your ingredient scores are strong (40+) but Integration Score is low (under 25), you have capabilities that are not working together.

The Issue: You are working hard but not smart. Your ingredients exist in silos. They do not multiply each other.

WARNING SIGN #3: Everything Scored 7-8 Out of 10

If all 30 behaviors are scored in the 7-8 range, you likely inflated

your scores. The Issue: You are not being honest with yourself. Go back and rescore: "How often do I ACTUALLY do this?" not "How often do I THINK I do this?"

WARNING SIGN #4: Externalizing Change

If you scored yourself high but believe your TEAM needs work, you are externalizing. The Issue: Remember the accountability paradox. "I\'m fine, everyone else needs to change" is self-deception.

WHAT TO DO WITH YOUR SCORES

Your Kryptonite Scorecard is not just diagnostic — it is directional. It tells you exactly where to focus.

ACTION #1: Identify Your Weakest Ingredient

Look at your five ingredient totals. Which scored lowest? That is your starting point.

Why: Your Integration Score is limited by your weakest ingredient. Strengthening it creates immediate impact.

ACTION #2: Pick ONE Behavior to Improve

Within your weakest ingredient, identify the ONE behavior you scored lowest. That is your Week 1 focus.

Example: If SPEED is your weakest ingredient (score: 32) and behavior #11 scored 4/10 ("I iterate and improve quickly"), focus there first.

ACTION #3: Deploy Using Chapter 9 90-Day Plan

Turn to Chapter 9 and follow the week-by-week deployment framework. Apply it to the ONE behavior you identified.

Outcome: In 90 days, retake this assessment. Your score in that ingredient should improve by 5-10 points. Your Integration Score should improve as well.

ACTION #4: Retake This Assessment Every 90 Days

Leadership is a skill that demands ongoing practice. Track your progress.

- 90 days: Reassess to measure progress
- 180 days: Reassess again to confirm sustainable change
- 365 days: Full reassessment to measure transformation

The difference between professionals who survive disruption and those who get displaced is not knowledge. It is deployment.

Those prepared need not fear the forces at work.

. . .

WHY HIGHER KRYPTONITE SCORES PRODUCE BETTER OUTCOMES

This assessment is not an academic exercise. The five ingredients measured here — IDEAS, SPEED, TALENT, DISTINCTION, and LEADERSHIP AT ALL LEVELS — are the specific human capabilities that 27 years of research and practice inside Fortune

50 organizations consistently link to superior individual and organizational performance.

Here is what the evidence shows:

Professionals who score higher on IDEAS:

- Are identified by their organizations as innovation leaders at significantly higher rates than peers
- Receive more discretionary resources, visibility, and advancement opportunities
- Are retained at higher rates during restructuring because they are associated with growth rather than maintenance
- Report higher job satisfaction and lower anxiety about AI displacement — because they are building the future rather than defending the past

Professionals who score higher on SPEED:

- Complete initiatives faster, which compounds over time into a significant career and organizational advantage
- Are perceived by leadership as more decisive and trustworthy with larger responsibilities
- Are less likely to be bypassed by AI systems — because SPEED in humans is about judgment and decision-making, not processing, and judgment remains the human advantage

Professionals who score higher on TALENT:

- Demonstrate stronger team performance outcomes — their multiplier effect is measurable
- Build networks that become career assets during disruption, when relationships matter more than resumes
- Score significantly higher on 'irreplaceability' ratings in 360-degree feedback — colleagues and managers identify them as people the organization cannot afford to lose

Professionals who score higher on DISTINCTION:

- Command higher compensation at every career stage — distinction is directly correlated with earning power
- Are promoted into new roles created specifically for them, rather than competing for existing positions
- Are the first people clients, colleagues, and leaders think of for high-visibility opportunities — not because they marketed themselves aggressively, but because they made their value unmistakable

Professionals who score higher on LEADERSHIP AT ALL LEVELS:

- Are disproportionately represented in organizations that successfully navigate major disruption
- Create measurable culture effects — teams with high-LEADERSHIP professionals demonstrate higher engagement, lower turnover, and faster execution
- Remain valuable across role changes, industry shifts, and organizational restructuring because leadership is portable in a way that technical skills are not

The Integration Effect

The most significant finding across 27 years is this: professionals who score high on all five ingredients — and whose Integration Score reflects those capabilities working together — do not merely perform better. They operate in a different category entirely.

Integration is not additive. It is multiplicative. Five strong ingredients working together do not produce five times the result. They produce exponential differentiation that competitors cannot easily replicate — because they cannot copy a system. They can only copy components.

The professionals in this category are not immune to disruption. No one is. But they are consistently the ones who land on the right side of it — the ones organizations compete to retain, the ones who find opportunity where others find threat, the ones whose careers look completely different five years from now in the best possible way.

That is what high Kryptonite scores actually mean. Not a number on a page. A fundamentally different relationship with the future.

· · ·

THE FULL KRYPTONITE ASSESSMENT™

Going Beyond the Self-Assessment

The Kryptonite Scorecard in this appendix is your starting point. It gives you your self-assessment baseline — an honest picture of where you stand today based on your own perception of your behaviors.

But here is something important to keep in mind: over 27 years, I have consistently observed that professionals score themselves 30 to 40 percent higher than their colleagues score them. Not because they are dishonest. Because we see our intentions. Others see our behaviors.

Your self-assessment is valuable. It is also incomplete.

The Full Kryptonite Assessment™ — available at realmikeevans. com — takes the diagnostic to the next level with four capabilities the printed scorecard cannot provide:

1. Observer Feedback (360-Degree Assessment). Colleagues, direct reports, managers, and peers rate you on the same 30 behaviors you just rated yourself. The gap between how you see yourself and how others experience you is where the most significant development insight lives. It is also the most honest measure of your actual current capability.

2. Visual Reporting Dashboard. Your results are presented in a professional visual report that includes bar graphs comparing your self-scores against observer averages for each behavior, percentile ranking charts showing where you stand relative to other professionals who have completed the assessment, circular progress indicators for each ingredient showing your current score against the maximum, behavior ranking tables identifying your most and least frequent behaviors, and standard deviation data showing the consistency of observer responses across raters.

3. Organizational Benchmarking. For teams and organizations that deploy the Full Assessment across a group, reporting includes aggregate scores by team, department, or division — showing where collective integration is strong and where organizational capability gaps exist. This is the data that drives meaningful leadership development investment rather than generic training programs.

4. Longitudinal Tracking. The digital platform tracks your scores across multiple assessment cycles — 90 days, 180 days, 12 months — so you can see your actual growth over time. The visual trend data is motivating in a way that a single snapshot never can be.

The self-assessment in this book gives you the map. The Full Kryptonite Assessment gives you the GPS — with real-time feedback, visual reporting, and the perspective of the people who experience your leadership every day.

For Organizations and Teams

The Full Kryptonite Assessment™ is available for organizational deployment, with options for team-level reporting, facilitated debrief sessions, and integration with leadership development programs. Licensing options are available for HR leaders, learning and development professionals, executive coaches, and consultants who want to deploy the assessment with their clients and teams.

How to Access

Visit realmikeevans.com/scorecard to access the digital assessment, learn about organizational licensing, and explore workshop and keynote programs built around the Kryptonite framework.

For organizational inquiries:
mike@realmikeevans.com • 412.616.6115

· · ·

Those prepared need not fear the forces at work.

90-DAY DEPLOYMENT WORKSHEETS

These worksheets are your implementation companion to Chapter 9. Use them week by week. Write in this book. Dog-ear the pages. This is not a document to read and shelve, it is a tool to use.

The framework is simple. Each week has a focus, a set of actions, and a space to record what actually happened. The discipline of writing it down is not administrative. It is the difference between intention and deployment.

. . .

Before You Begin: Your Baseline Assessment

Complete this before Week 1. You need a starting point to measure progress against.

Date completed: ______________________________

Your Kryptonite Scorecard Summary

Transfer your scores from Appendix A:

IDEAS score: ______ / 60

SPEED score: ______ / 60

TALENT score: ______ / 60

DISTINCTION score: ______ / 60

LEADERSHIP score: ______ / 60

TOTAL score: _____ / 300
INTEGRATION score: _____ / 50

Your Starting Point

My LOWEST scoring ingredient: __________________

My lowest single behavior (number and description):

____

My HIGHEST scoring ingredient: __________________

My Integration Score tells me:

____

Your 90-Day Commitment

Write it in your own words. What specifically do you commit to changing in the next 90 days?

____

____

____

My accountability partner for this 90 days: ____________

Date of first accountability check-in: ________________

. . .

WEEKS 1–2: Establish Your Baseline

Focus: Honest self-assessment and identification of your highest-leverage starting point. Do not skip this. The entire 90 days is calibrated from what you discover here.

Week 1, Day 1

Action: Complete your full Kryptonite Scorecard (Appendix A). Enter scores above.

- ☐ Scorecard completed
- ☐ Scores transferred to the Baseline section above
- ☐ Integration Score calculated

Week 1, Days 2–5

Actions: Identify your lowest-scoring ingredient and diagnose why.

- ☐ Identified my lowest-scoring ingredient
- ☐ Written three specific examples of how this weakness has cost me in the past year
- ☐ Identified one person who excels in this area and scheduled 30 minutes with them

The three ways this weakness has cost me:

1. ____

____

2. ____

____

3. ____

____

THE PERSON I WILL LEARN FROM:

Name: _______________ Date scheduled: _______________

What I want to learn from them:

____

Week 2

Actions: Map your current initiatives against the five ingredients. Find the disconnects.

- ☐ Mapped current initiatives against all five ingredients
- ☐ Identified the biggest disconnect (where ingredients work against each other)
- ☐ Chosen ONE integration to fix first

My current initiatives mapped to ingredients:

IDEAS initiatives currently underway:

____

SPEED initiatives currently underway:

____

TALENT initiatives currently underway:

____

DISTINCTION initiatives currently underway:

____

LEADERSHIP initiatives currently underway:

____

My biggest disconnect (two ingredients not talking to each other):

____

____

The ONE integration I will fix first:

____

____

OUTCOME after Week 2: You know exactly where you stand, what's broken, and what to fix first.

My Week 2 Outcome — write what you actually know now:

____

____

____

• • •

WEEKS 3–4: Quick Wins

Focus: Early momentum. Do not start with the hardest changes. Start with wins that prove the system works and build your confidence to go further.

Week 3

Actions: Three specific moves that create visible progress.

☐ Implemented ONE speed improvement — eliminated one approval step, meeting, or bottleneck

☐ Launched ONE idea I have been sitting on — prototyped in one day, tested within the week
☐ Had ONE conversation I have been avoiding

MY WEEK 3 ACTIONS — SPECIFICS:

Speed improvement I eliminated:

____

Result: ____

Idea I launched:

____

Result: ____

Conversation I had:

____

Result: ____

Week 4

Actions: Claim your wins. Build on them. Schedule the next three.

☐ Documented my three wins from Week 3
☐ Shared them with my team or manager — claimed credit, built reputation
☐ Identified the next three quick wins and scheduled them

My three Week 3 wins (written for sharing):

1. ____

2. ____

3. ____

My next three quick wins and target dates:

1. _______________________________ By: _________________

2. _______________________________ By: _________________

3. _______________________________ By: _________________

OUTCOME after Week 4: Visible progress. Proof that this works. Momentum.

My Week 4 Outcome — what momentum have I built?

____

____

. . .

WEEKS 5–8: Build Your Integration

Focus: Now you tackle the integration you identified in Week 2. This is where isolated capability becomes a connected system.

Weeks 5–6: Connect Two Ingredients

Actions: Design and launch one initiative that leverages two ingredients simultaneously.

- ☐ Identified the two ingredients I am connecting
- ☐ Designed one initiative that leverages both
- ☐ Launched the initiative

The two ingredients I am connecting:

Ingredient 1: _________________ Ingredient 2: _____________

My integration initiative — what exactly am I doing?

____

____

____

How this connects both ingredients:

____

____

Launch date: _____________________ First check-in date: _______

Weeks 7–8: Test and Adjust

Actions: Measure, learn, adjust. Document what you discover.

☐ Launched my integration initiative
☐ Measured results weekly
☐ Adjusted based on what is working and what is not
☐ Documented lessons learned

Week 7 results — what is working?

____

____

Week 7 results — what is not working?

____

____

Adjustments I made:

____

____

Week 8 results — measurable evidence the integration is working:

____

____

OUTCOME after Week 8: One working integration. Proof that the system works.

My Week 8 Outcome — what is the evidence?

____

____

. . .

WEEKS 9–12: Scale and Embed

Focus: Expand what is working. Make integration permanent — not a project you are running, but how you operate.

Weeks 9–10: Add a Third Ingredient

Actions: Extend your working integration to include a third ingredient.

- ☐ Identified the third ingredient to connect to my working integration
- ☐ Trained one other person on my integration approach
- ☐ Launched the expanded integration

My working integration (from Weeks 5–8):

____

The third ingredient I am adding: _______________________

How I am connecting it:

____

____

The person I trained on my approach:

Name: _________________________ Date: _________________________

What I taught them:

____

Weeks 11–12: Make It Standard Operating Procedure

Actions: Document, share, institutionalize. The goal is that this integration survives without you driving it.

☐ Documented my integration as a repeatable process
☐ Shared results with my team or organization
☐ Built it into how I operate going forward
☐ Scheduled my next 90-day cycle

My integration documented as a repeatable process:

Step 1: ____

Step 2: ____

Step 3: ____

Step 4: ____

Results I shared and with whom:

____

____

My next 90-day cycle start date: _______________________________

OUTCOME after Week 12: Integration is now how you work — not something you are trying to do.

My Week 12 Outcome — what has permanently changed?

____

____

____

. . .

Weekly Accountability Tracker

Use this tracker every Monday morning. Fifteen minutes. Three questions. No exceptions.

The questions never change: What did I commit to? What did I actually do? What is my commitment this week?

Week 1

Date: ____

What I committed to last week:

____

What I actually did:

____

____

My commitment this week:

____

____

Week 2

Date: ____

What I committed to last week:

____

What I actually did:

____

____

My commitment this week:

____

____

Week 3

Date: ____

What I committed to last week:

____

What I actually did:

____

____

My commitment this week:

____

____

Week 4

Date: ____

What I committed to last week:

____

What I actually did:

____

____

My commitment this week:

____

____

Week 5

Date: ____

What I committed to last week:

____

What I actually did:

____

____

My commitment this week:

____

____

Week 6

Date: ____

What I committed to last week:

____

What I actually did:

____

____

My commitment this week:

____

____

Week 7

Date: ____

What I committed to last week:

____

What I actually did:

____

____

My commitment this week:

____

____

Week 8

Date: ____

What I committed to last week:

____

What I actually did:

____

____

My commitment this week:

____

____

Week 9

Date: ____

What I committed to last week:

____

What I actually did:

____

____

My commitment this week:

____

____

Week 10

Date: _______________________________________

What I committed to last week:

____

What I actually did:

____

____

My commitment this week:

____

____

Week 11

Date: _______________________________________

What I committed to last week:

____

What I actually did:

____

____

My commitment this week:

____

____

Week 12

Date: ____

What I committed to last week:

____

What I actually did:

____

____

My commitment this week:

____

____

. . .

Day 90: Reassessment

Retake the full Kryptonite Scorecard from Appendix A. Enter your new scores below and compare to your baseline.

Date of reassessment: _______________________________

Your New Scores

IDEAS score:　　　　　______ / 60　(was ______ / 60)

SPEED score:　　　　　______ / 60　(was ______ / 60)

TALENT score:　　　　______ / 60　(was ______ / 60)

DISTINCTION score:　______ / 60　(was ______ / 60)

LEADERSHIP score:　　______ / 60　(was ______ / 60)

TOTAL score:　　　　　______ / 300　(was ______ / 300)

INTEGRATION score:　______ / 50　(was ______ / 50)

What Changed

My biggest score improvement: _______________________

The behavior that changed the most:

____

What surprised me about my results:

____

____

What Stays Hard

The ingredient still lowest: _______________________

Why I think it is still difficult:

____

____

My next 90-day focus area:

____

____

Share Your Results

The professionals who track and share their progress are the ones who sustain it. Tell your accountability partner your scores. Tell your manager what changed. If you are willing, share it publicly.

The discipline of measurement is itself a behavior — and it belongs under LEADERSHIP AT ALL LEVELS.

. . .

Obstacle Response Guide

When deployment stalls — and it will stall at some point — use this guide. Write down what happened and what you did about it.

Obstacle 1: "I don't have time for this."

Response: This plan requires 2–4 hours per week. Identify one meeting, one report, or one activity that adds less value than your Kryptonite development. Eliminate or reduce it. Protect the time.

What I eliminated to make time:

____

____

Obstacle 2: "My organization won't support this."

Response: You do not need organizational permission to develop IDEAS, increase your SPEED, build TALENT, create DISTINCTION, or demonstrate LEADERSHIP. Start with what you control. Prove it works. Others will notice.

What I started without permission:

____

____

Obstacle 3: "What if I fail?"

Response: You are already failing if you are standing still while disruption accelerates. The only real failure is not attempting. Reframe: every attempt teaches you something. Adjust and try again.

The attempt I made and what I learned:

____

____

Obstacle 4: A crisis derailed my deployment.

Response: Crises are the test of commitment, not the excuse for abandonment. What is the minimum you can do this week to keep the thread alive? One behavior. Fifteen minutes. Do not let a crisis become a full stop.

What I did to keep the thread alive:

____

____

Obstacle 5: Leadership changed or stopped supporting this.

Response: The Kryptonite framework is yours, not your organization's. IDEAS, SPEED, TALENT, DISTINCTION, and LEADERSHIP are personal capabilities. You own them regardless of what leadership does or does not prioritize.

How I maintained ownership regardless:

____

____

. . .

These worksheets do not make the work easier. They make the work visible. And visible work is accountable work.

Fill them out. Come back to them. Update them when things change. Share them with your accountability partner.

Ninety days from now, the professionals who completed these pages will have something the ones who did not will not have: evidence. Evidence that they deployed, not just learned. Evidence that they changed, not just intended to.

The difference between professionals who survive disruption and those who get displaced is not knowledge. It is deployment.

Those prepared need not fear the forces at work.

ACKNOWLEDGMENTS

This book represents 27 years of learning, and I'm deeply grateful to everyone who contributed to that journey.

To my wife, Despina: Thank you for your patience during countless early mornings and late nights of writing. Your honest feedback on every draft made this book immeasurably better. More importantly, your unwavering support of my work, even when it meant disrupted weekends and missed dinners, made it possible. You've been my partner in every sense of the word.

To my sons Nick and Zack, and my stepchildren, Brady and Brooke: You inspire me more than you know. Watching you grow up in this rapidly changing world, seeing your curiosity about technology and your adaptability to change, reminds me daily why this work matters. The future I'm writing about is the one you'll inherit. I hope this book helps make it a better one.

To Tom Peters, Dr. Stephen Covey, Dr. John Kotter, Jim Kouzes, and Barry Posner: Working alongside you shaped not just my career but my understanding of how real change happens in organizations. You taught me to see beyond theory to the messy, beautiful reality of human behavior. Your influence is woven throughout every page of this book.

To the thousands of leaders and teams I've had the privilege to work with over nearly three decades: You are the real authors of this book. Every story, every insight, every framework emerged from our work together. You taught me what actually works, not just what sounds good in theory. Your willingness to share your challenges, your failures, and your breakthroughs gave me the raw material to create something useful for others facing similar struggles.

Special thanks to the 34 Fortune 50 companies who trusted me to help navigate their most critical transformations. Working at the scale and complexity you operate at forced me to develop frameworks that could withstand real-world pressure. The lessons learned at Intel, Apple, PepsiCo, Caterpillar, and the other industry-leading organizations I've served made this book possible.

To the audiences who've attended my keynotes and workshops over the years: Your questions challenged me. Your feedback sharpened my thinking. Your stories enriched my understanding. Every presentation taught me something new about how to communicate complex ideas in ways that land and stick. This book is more accessible because of you.

To the colleagues and early readers who reviewed drafts and provided candid feedback: Your willingness to tell me what wasn't working, not just what was, elevated this manuscript from good to something I'm proud to share with the world. Thank you for your honesty and your time.

Finally, to everyone navigating the uncertainty of rapid change: This book exists because you needed it. Your courage to face disruption rather than deny it, to adapt rather than resist, to lead rather than hide, inspired every word. The world needs more people like you. Thank you for choosing to become distinct rather than extinct.

ABOUT THE AUTHOR

Mike Evans isn't another AI expert who discovered it in 2023 and rebranded. He's the speaker who's been tracking the seven-force convergence disrupting work since 1995, with AI as the most recent accelerant, not the original threat.

The difference: 27 years, not 27 months.

For nearly three decades, Mike has held executive leadership roles at three of the world's premier organizational transformation firms: Kotter International, FranklinCovey, and Tom Peters Company. These weren't consulting positions where he advised from the sidelines. He was in the room when billion-dollar decisions were made, working directly with Dr. John Kotter, Dr. Stephen Covey, Tom Peters, and Jim Kouzes to execute transformation with Intel, Apple, PepsiCo, Caterpillar, and 30 other Fortune 50 companies.

The results were measurable. NetApp achieved 175% equity growth. The U.S. Army Aviation Center transformed pilot training under severe budget constraints. Intel accelerated decision-making from weeks to days. These weren't theoretical frameworks, they were operational systems that delivered outcomes when the stakes were highest.

While most consultants were treating the internet as a novelty in the late 1990s, Mike was already helping Fortune 50 companies navigate what he recognized as the beginning of a fundamental shift. Over the following decades, he watched as globalization, outsourcing, automation, robotics, and digital disruption each emerged as new forces threatening organizational stability. He didn't just observe these changes—he developed frameworks to help people and organizations master them.

What Mike calls the "7-Sided Pincer Movement" didn't start with AI. It started with six other disruptive forces, each powerful enough on its own to obsolete careers and companies. AI didn't create this threat. It amplified it. It accelerated it. It made the stakes exponentially higher. That's why Mike's approach is fundamentally different from the sudden surge of self-proclaimed AI experts. He's not reacting to a trend. He's continuing work he's been doing for 27 years, now armed with urgent data about how quickly the future is arriving.

Mike's expertise isn't theoretical. It's operational. He doesn't just identify problems or paint apocalyptic scenarios. He delivers the defense. The "5-Ingredient Kryptonite Defense" framework presented in this book—IDEAS, SPEED, TALENT, DISTINCTION, LEADERSHIP AT ALL LEVELS, is the distillation of thousands of hours working with 34 Fortune 50 companies. These aren't abstract concepts. They're battle-tested strategies that have helped real people and real organizations not just survive disruption but dominate because of it.

As an award-winning keynote speaker, Mike delivers 40-60 presentations annually to corporate audiences and major conferences, translating complex future-of-work challenges into immediately actionable frameworks. **His approach combines visceral storytelling with proprietary frameworks that leaders implement Monday morning**, not someday when conditions are perfect.

His book, Distinct or Extinct: Future-Proofing People and Organizations in the Age of AI, distills 27 years of pattern recognition into a practical framework for professionals and organizations navigating AI disruption. It includes the Kryptonite Scorecard™, a proprietary 30-behavior diagnostic assessment available in the book and digitally at realmikeevans.com/scorecard.

His signature message:
"Those prepared need not fear the forces at work."

Learn more at **realmikeevans.com**